*inner fitness*

# *inner*

# FITNESS

## THE SIX-STEP PROGRAM TO ACHIEVE A

## FIT MIND FOR FAST DECISIONS

## VICTOR DISHY

**DOUBLEDAY**

NEW YORK  LONDON  TORONTO  SYDNEY  AUCKLAND

*Illustrations by Jackie Aher*

PUBLISHED BY DOUBLEDAY

a division of Bantam Doubleday Dell Publishing Group, Inc.

666 Fifth Avenue, New York, New York 10103

DOUBLEDAY and the portrayal of an anchor
with a dolphin are trademarks of Doubleday,
a division of Bantam Doubleday Dell
Publishing Group, Inc.

Library of Congress Cataloging-in-Publication Data

Dishy, Victor.
    Inner fitness : the six step program to achieve a fit mind for fast
decisions / by Victor Dishy.
        p.   cm.
    1. Success—Psychological aspects.   2. Mental discipline.
3. Decision-making.   4. Conduct of life.   I. Title.
BF637.S8D445   1990
158′.1—dc20                                        90-30393
                                                        CIP

ISBN 978-0-385-50689-2

Printed in the United States of America

146484122

These "Tools for Living" Can Develop Your "Inner Fitness"—and Change Your Life!

1—The Drop of Elmer's Glue

2—The Bells

3—The Circle and Dot

4—The North Star

5—The Clock

6—The Bow Tie

*How do you use them?*

*When do you use them?*

*Which one do you use?*

*What can you achieve with them?*

The answers are in the help-giving pages of this unique, life-enhancing book that offers a program for mental and emotional health and happiness that really works!

To be nobody—but—yourself in a world which is doing its best, night and day, to make you everybody else—means to fight the hardest battle which any human being can fight; and never stop fighting.

e. e. cummings

*To Amy and Nissim,*

*who against great odds*

*strove to maintain an*

*independence of spirit*

# ACKNOWLEDGMENTS

When I was quite young, I believed that writers had magic pens out of which wonderful words flowed. In writing this book, I learned differently. I learned the magic is in the rewriting. And the magic is in the grace with which others share their thoughts and talents. Thanks to Sharon Kingston, McKee Anderson, Joan Groves, Terry Richards, Ken Husney, Joan Hobbs, Monique Yellin, Barry Leshner, Ken Dressler, Sara Blackburn, Ralph Brody, along with so many others, who by their willingness and candor helped shape my program.

I am grateful to my agent, Connie Clausen, for her tireless efforts on my behalf and to my editor, Loretta Barrett, who steadfastly believed in the spirit and message of *Inner Fitness*.

I owe a particular debt of gratitude to my wife, Zaida, for her patience and for her uncanny ability to know when I had something to say or was merely spouting words. I owe much to Andrew Karp. I owe Andrew a special thanks for his understanding of the program, along with his literary skills.

# INNER FITNESS

# FOREWORD: TALK IS NOT ENOUGH

I don't know about you, but I've had it with books that take four hundred pages to tell me that I have a problem and then offer no solution. I also take a dim view of books that tell us how to dress, act, negotiate, or feel but offer no realistic program for changing our entrenched, lifelong habits. Such books may strengthen our resolve momentarily but fall short when faced with the test of long-term and day-to-day decision making. Just as a white-hot iron rod cools soon after being removed from the fire, so do we snap back to our old ways as soon as we put down these books.

Most books on how to live more effective lives prove ineffectual because they offer nothing more than ad hoc lists of advice that are not part of an integrated, holistic system working on all levels of thinking and feeling. Such psychological advice, too often passing itself as "scientific," neglects the spiritual and intuitive side of man.

**When it comes to improving the way we function and com-**

municate with others, we must change at the core to rediscover our true, inner selves. To translate good ideas into practice requires a total, holistic program plus commitment, concentration, and conditioning. Only then will we be able to function on our own, spontaneously and naturally, without the aid of gimmicks or manipulative behavioral ploys.

In this book I present a complete regimen for conditioning the mind and the emotions. A regimen that affects our innermost being and provides us workable techniques for obtaining the peak performance I call Inner Fitness.

*In selling, unless you close the sale and come back with the check you're merely a conversationalist.* Thus, in devising the Inner Fitness Program, and testing it through a series of extensive workshops, I have sought to galvanize you to take actions leading to beneficial changes in your lives.

What follows then is an effort intended to make you a richer human being. I will do my best to sell you not only on the ideas behind Inner Fitness but on the need to apply the program's various conditioning excercises. Put my step-by-step plan to work and you will learn to live creatively and be ready and eager to take chances, face change, and grasp those fleeting opportunities for success and accomplishment that appear all too infrequently in our lives.

# INTRODUCTION: INNER FITNESS AND THE TOOLS FOR LIVING—HOW TO USE THIS BOOK

**C**entral to the Inner Fitness Program is the premise that being true to oneself is the most productive, realistic, and pragmatic way to live our lives. Whatever our goals and objectives—whether to succeed in business or actualize our personal potential—we must effect a symmetry between what we sense is right for us and how we go about living our lives on a day-to-day basis. The Tools for Living will help us develop that symmetry.

The Tools consist of six different but interrelated living skills, each represented by a visual cue and each supported by examples. Each of the Tools contains a solid, practical piece of advice on how we can improve and retrain our thinking, attitudes, and emotions.

At the end of each chapter is a set of what I call "Conditioning Exercises." These specific mental and emotional drills are intended to take the reader from theory to practice. They show how we can apply the tools to our own lives on a day-to-day basis and encourage us to practice making those small changes in our lives that will prepare us to handle major decisions.

I suggest the following step-by-step procedure as a way to achieve the greatest benefit from the Inner Fitness Program.

## Phase I: Inner Receptivity

Inner Fitness begins with a personal commitment to ourselves made in the privacy of our own thoughts. Take a quiet moment to confirm that you are receptive to and ready for change. Before you can begin conditioning your mind and emotions, you must affirm your desire to embrace Creative Living and the "I Choose" life.

## Phase II: The Total Program

Read through the entire book at least once. The first reading will give you a feel for the whole program and allow you to place each Tool in its context. The Tools are presented in a developmental progression, increasing in complexity and moving from the internal to the external, from silence to speech, from the personal to the social. They will lead you from nonverbal to verbal skills, from the avoidance of errors to the discovery of positive directions. They will put you in touch with your nonverbal self, make you aware that you are choosing your own way, lead you to the realization that you must follow your spiritual core, alert you to change, and, hone your skill at communicating with others. Although the Tools are presented in this sequence, when it comes to applying these Tools to our lives, they need not be used in any fixed order.

## Phase III: The Conditioning Exercises

On second reading, pause to do the Conditioning Exercises. Spend a week working on each Tool. Practice applying it to your life. Emphasize those exercises that hit home. When your life is most hectic and pressured is the precise time to use the Tools for Living.

After you've worked through the Conditioning Exercises, recall the Tools' variety of uses. Then, at a given moment, in a particular situation, use whichever one seems most appropriate and effective. Use the Work Sheet approach described in Chapter 10—listing all the Tools and applying them one by one, in order—to help you solve a particularly thorny problem. Or, alternately, use the Tools *after* you've made a decision or been in a conflict as a kind of therapy to help you understand and work through a problem area.

## Phase IV: Forward Momentum

Although the Inner Fitness Program can be completed in a matter of weeks, it is not intended to be a quick, finite fix. It is, instead, an ongoing program that will continue to help you once you've mastered and internalized the message of the Tools. As with any skill, there will always remain room for improvement. Keep returning to the Tools to discover new applications of their power. The more we use them, the more insight we will gain into ourselves and the more forward momentum we will achieve in our lives.

# HOW THE INNER FITNESS PROGRAM CAME INTO BEING

One Fall afternoon in the early eighties, I began to review the turning points in my life, reliving my major and seemingly minor but actually critical decisions. Although I'd had my ups and downs, overall I felt generally fortunate. Suddenly, something clicked. From the many images, ideas, and experiences that came to mind, a pattern seemed to emerge.

I realized that I achieved my greatest successes when I broke with tradition and followed my spontaneous, creative urges. When I opted for security and allowed my decisions to be guided by fears and pressures, by propriety and circumstance, I committed errors in judgment and achieved only pedestrian results.

When I trusted my feelings and intuitions, and made them a full and equal partner with my rational side, I felt a sense of joy and self-respect. This insight led to a second realization: I had more power over my own life than I had ever dreamed possible. I was not controlled by circumstance, environment, luck, or a host of outside factors. On the contrary, at every moment, *I* was choosing my own way, deciding which path to take and which decisions to make. *I* was creating my own life and choosing my own destiny.

In reviewing my moments of personal fulfillment as well as my business successes in marketing, training sales personnel, negotiating, and communicating, I thought about the method by which I assimilated information and arrived at decisions. I had spent years studying and conducting workshops in a theory of communication and perception developed by Alfred Korzybski, the eminent semanticist and author of *Science and Sanity*. His system of thought, called General Semantics or GS, was designed to lead us away from an outdated way of thinking to fresh, new approaches more in keeping with modern science and with nature. What I learned about people, however, didn't come out of a textbook. It came out of my life. Through my personal and business experience, I learned profound lessons about human nature and developed a repertoire of mental attitudes and self-imposed rules. Here again a pattern emerged.

I realized that, both consciously and unconsciously, I had been using a variety of tools and techniques to help me make sound judgments. I felt they had universal application and could offer others the opportunity to turn living into not only a skill but an exciting personal voyage. In the pages that follow, I would like to share those insights with you.

*part* 1

GETTING
STARTED

# INNER FITNESS: A MENTAL AND EMOTIONAL CONDITIONING PROGRAM

Without a doubt, the 1980s has been the decade of physical fitness. From jogging to weight training, from low-impact aerobics to walking, all of us have been made more aware of the need for and the benefits of exercise, conditioning, and proper nutrition. We have changed our diets and arranged our schedules to make exercise a part of our daily regimen. But what good are leaner, healthier bodies if our minds and emotions are unfit?

Too many of us today are split in two. Our minds and bodies are out of sync. We lead dual lives, disguising our real selves, behaving one way at work and another at home. As a result of the lack of harmony between what we do and what we feel and believe, we squander our energies and diminish our productivity.

Now is the time for us to reconnect our bodies and our minds, to reorient and reintegrate our internal programming, and to progress beyond training only our bodies.

We know that we have to exercise regularly and eat the right foods if we want to achieve a feeling of physical or outer fitness. We also need a program to stretch our minds and build our emotional stamina if we want to develop the skills necessary to achieve Inner Fitness. This means living a life of personal choice, avoiding a host of unnecessary traps and errors in our thinking, and making the most of our potentials.

Inner Fitness is a down-to-earth mental conditioning program designed to help us retrain our minds and emotions. Made up of six easy-to-understand-and-remember Tools for Living, each accompanied by appropriate exercises, the program trains us to shed self-defeating behavior patterns and replace them with natural and functional response patterns. Requiring no special equipment and taking up no more than a few minutes a day, Inner Fitness helps us overcome our biases. By preventing us from jumping to unwarranted conclusions, by teaching us to respond appropriately to changing problems, and by urging us to follow our fascination, this program conditions us to tackle the tough decisions that life presents.

**Applying the Tools for Living is similar to moving through a weight-training circuit.** Just as each station or exercise on a circuit performs a specific function and works a specific muscle in order to tone and build the entire body, so, too, the Inner Fitness Program offers a circuit of mental cues and exercises to help us stretch, tone, and build our emotional and intellectual strengths. When we successfully undergo Inner Fitness training, the feeling of euphoria (from realizing a creative drive or discovering and acting upon a fresh option) will easily match the runner's high or the weight lifter's muscle glow.

Through Inner Fitness, we will learn how to live happily in accordance with our personal values and instincts. I am not, however, advising anyone to sacrifice life's material comforts. On the contrary, it is my conviction, based upon my personal and business experience, that *being true to oneself, far from being an idealistic pipe dream, is actually the most pragmatic path to success.* **This simple truth appears to be the most well-kept secret of our times.**

By showing us how to realize our dreams and make sound, honest decisions that are true to our innermost selves, Inner Fitness provides us with the conditioning needed to harness and unleash our "spirituality." It prepares us to make that shift in paradigms called for by Fritjof

Capra in his book *The Turning Point* and shows us how to fulfill our potential and achieve the self-actualization championed by Abraham Maslow. My hope is that the Inner Fitness Program may help provide the missing link between reason and spirit, between the Old and the New Age, between the bottom-line mentality and the new people-oriented management style, that we will need to function in the future. By conditioning us to change at the core and function in harmony with ourselves and our environment, Inner Fitness will help us all to fulfill our dreams and potentials, thus lifting our human spirit and leading us, at peace with ourselves, into the twenty-first century.

TURNING AN
"I SHOULD" LIFE
INTO AN
"I CHOOSE" LIFE

Why do some people who seem to have everything feel as if they have nothing?

With a shock of red hair and a rosy complexion, Ralph B. looks and acts the part of a bright, young thirty-three-year-old account supervisor at a New York City advertising agency. His clients love him, his fellow workers enjoy his razor-sharp wit, he lives in a comfortable Upper West Side apartment. Every morning before work, he jogs several miles around the reservoir in Central Park, and every other evening he pumps iron at the New York Health and Racquet Club. On weekends, he and his wife prepare gourmet food for their friends and attend Off-Broadway shows. In the summer, they rent a spacious house on Shelter Island. Yet Ralph despairs of his life.

Mary H. is in her late thirties, petite and attractive, with a secure job as a secretary in a small architectural firm in the suburbs of Boston. She has a modicum of responsibility and gets along well with the office staff. Divorced three years now from her alcoholic husband, Mary raises two well-behaved teen-agers, loves the outdoors, and is currently dating an older man, an engineer, who has asked her to marry him. Although convinced that he would make a good husband and father, she still can't bring herself to say "yes." Mary cries often and is confused by her deep feelings of restlessness and malaise.

Do *you* churn inside with anger, frustration, and unhappiness even though your life seems secure and comfortable on the outside?

Are you merely going through the motions of living?

Do you rely on drugs or alcohol to get you through the week?

Are you bored with your mate or your job?

Do you find your work so aggravating and unchallenging that you live only for the weekends?

Are you tortured by the demands of a boss you can never satisfy?

Do you spend so much time on your work that you never have time to enjoy what you earn?

Have you had your fill of psychology, technology, and rationalism but don't know where else to turn?

Do you curse against the gods, the fates, the government, or your parents, holding them responsible for your bad luck and your lot in life?

"Where are you rushing?" a man once asked his friend. "I don't know," the friend answered, "I'm too busy trying to get there."

> **Too often we rush through our lives without stopping to consult our instincts or daring to act on our dreams.**

Ralph B. secretly despises advertising and hates himself for selling out. With a doctorate in English and a love for art and literature, Ralph wants to be a writer but, out of fear and insecurity, locks himself into a job, a salary, and a lifestyle that he can't bring himself to shake. He keeps his body fit but never dreams there is anything he can do to put himself into a state of mental and emotional fitness.

Mary H. feels as if her life is over, tied down and boxed in by a menial, unchallenging desk job. Compelled to sacrifice herself for her children, afraid of spending the rest of her life alone, she assumes she has no choice but to marry a man whom she doesn't love. Secretly, Mary wants to move to California, finish college, and become a forest ranger. But she buries her dreams, opting for what she perceives is security, and drags herself through her days and nights of loneliness, psychic pain, and frustration.

Ralph and Mary are underachievers in the business of living. They are typical of people who feel trapped by their life situations and whose emotional well-being is harmed by regrets, fears, frustrated dreams, and faulty perceptions. They are living "I Should" lives, doing what they think they *should* do rather than what they *want* to do. They are living their lives according to the dictates of society and propriety, rather than dynamically and creatively.

I was like that once. I felt the pressure, just as we all do. The pressure to hold on to a job or a mate (for fear we won't find another), to accept our lot in life, to avoid emotional risk and danger. We feel it from our parents, from our peers, from our bosses or clients—from the accumulated history of our experiences. When we succumb to the pressures of the "I Should" life, the future seems more a threat than an opportunity. Erecting defenses to protect against real and imagined dangers, we trust the opinions of others more than our own. Sacrificing our dreams in exchange for the illusion of security, we distort our perceptions and allow our creativity and spontaneity to be stifled. We let ourselves be motivated by fear.

Fear motivates all of us to action (or inaction). It is an appropriate response to certain life-threatening situations; however, many of the daily fears in our lives gnaw away at our souls and wreak havoc with our emotional landscape. Fear of poverty, loneliness, the unknown, fear of making a mistake, of not fitting in, of not living up to others' expectations drive us farther and farther away from ourselves and deeper and deeper into the painful paralysis of the "I Should" life.

In my conversations with potential investors over the years, the saddest and most common refrain I have heard is prefaced by "If only . . ." "If only I had bought that stock," "If only I had turned down that job," "If only I had lived my life differently." Out of fear of following our instincts, too many of us end up bemoaning our past and living with the anguish of eternal regret and unfulfilled dreams.

What a shame! What a waste! If we fear the future and feel as if our lives are over or out of control, no wonder our lives seem joyless. Lacking self-respect, we turn to drink, develop ulcers or even cancer, alienate our spouses and children, and seek psychiatric help. Little wonder that Ralph B. has begun using drugs or that Mary H. neglects her children and her housework.

For Ralph B. and Mary H., as with most of us, breaking free from the hidden power of the "I Should" life isn't just advisable; it's a matter of self-preservation.

Fortunately, an alternative exists: the "I Choose" life. And it begins with how we perceive ourselves and the world.

## CREATIVE VERSUS PREVENTIVE LIVING

**Living the "I Choose" life, we choose to risk instead of allowing ourselves to be guided by fear.** We try something new instead of playing it safe. Refusing to live by an already written scenario, we seek out the many options life holds out to us. Only by having the courage to explore, shift perspective, and take calculated risks do we take control of our own lives. In so doing, we move forward, evolve, and open ourselves to growth and opportunity. This willingness to take chances is the heart of the "I Choose" lifestyle; it is also the core of Creative rather than Preventive Living.

Preventive Living is reactive. It leads us to avoid problems at all costs, to become defensive, to wait passively for the world to make us a victim. We end up as helpless and frustrated as Ralph and Mary.

Creative Living, on the other hand, entails taking control of our own lives and striving to fulfill our deepest dreams. It means using our heart and our head to create new options. It means living the life we want for ourselves instead of passively letting ourselves be molded and frustrated by circumstance and the demands of others.

Of course, we all have to make compromises and trade-offs in order to get by. We all have bosses and spouses, landlords and laws, bills and obligations. And we are all influenced and somewhat crippled by fear and its cruel companion, "should." But in order to succeed, we must make a voluntary and dynamic compromise to adapt to the demands of a situation without sacrificing our identity, individuality, or independence. Our mental and emotional well-being, our Inner Fitness, depends on it. The trick is to know when that invisible line has been crossed and we must end a relationship, quit a job, or change a lifestyle pattern . . . or risk sinking deeper into the mire of "I Should."

---

*The "I Should" Lifestyle*
**Conform and adapt. Take risks only when I must.**

*The "I Choose" Lifestyle*
**Take risks. Conform and adapt only when I must.**

**The choice between them
is at the core of our existence.**

---

The way to shift ourselves from a Preventive to a Creative Lifestyle is to accept the premise, central to Inner Fitness, that living is a skill that can be developed through practice. By practicing and conditioning ourselves to solve our smaller problems, we build the emotional and mental readiness necessary to tackle the major decisions of our lives in a creative way.

## LIVING IS A SKILL

Recently, I was talking with an old tennis partner of mine, a mother of three who runs her own catering business. She was waving a book in her hand, beaming with pleasure. "Why so happy, Jamie?" I asked.

"I didn't finish a book," she responded exuberantly.

"That makes you happy?"

"You know how compulsive I am. Every time I start a book I feel compelled to finish it, even if I hate it. I was beginning to dread reading. Today, for the first time, I decided to stop reading a novel that was boring me to tears. I feel liberated! My whole perspective has changed!"

The same applies to life. If you don't like the life you're living, don't sit there gritting your teeth, cursing under your breath. Get up and walk out while there's still time to live the life you *want* to live.

"Sure, sure," you're muttering, "that's easy for you to say. You haven't got my problems or my bills or my aches and pains. Wanting to change your life and actually changing it are two very different things. 'Life's a bitch and then you die,' as the saying goes."

Not *my* saying. I believe that "Life is rich, and here's why." There is one huge assumption that stands in the way of our making that crucial change from a fear-driven life to one of challenge and excitement.

We assume that living comes naturally, that our behavior patterns are innate and unchangeable, that wise decision making is a God-given gift. How odd that we approach so complex a task as living in so naïve a fashion. While we wouldn't dream of operating even the most user-friendly personal computer without at least reading the instruction manual, we plow through life untrained for its complexities and pitfalls.

**Unlike animals who depend solely upon instinct for survival,** *human beings must learn how to respond to their environment.* We must learn how to make sound and productive choices. Living happily, productively, creatively doesn't come any more naturally than a crisp, spin serve in tennis or a muscular, well-toned body. Just look around you and see how many people are falling flat on their faces, embroiled in miserable relationships, making one bad decision after another, hating their jobs, bumbling their way through life. Without realizing it, such people fall into self-destructive behavior patterns driven by hidden learned responses.

Why leave our one opportunity for happiness and success to chance? Making the most of life—not merely existing or going through the motions of living—isn't an inborn trait or a knack, it's a skill and, as such, requires practice, training, and conditioning. And that's the good news. Because if living is a skill, it can be learned.

I'm not talking in the abstract. What I am talking about are the skills we need to make sound decisions, to choose the right mate and the right job, to lose weight or make an important investment. Too often, we sit back and let the world push us about as if we had no control. We let old, outmoded ideas and hidden assumptions latch onto us like pit bull terriers. We need to shake off the grip of stifling beliefs and take control of our own lives.

**The crucial first step on the road to a revitalized lifestyle is realizing that living well is *the* essential skill to master. Accept that concept and we're ready to explore the ways and means of living better through the application of the Inner Fitness Program.**

Are you facing an important business decision? Are you contemplating marriage, divorce, a job change? Are you in the throes of despair because your job frustrates you or you can't find a suitable romantic partner? Are you unsure of what you want to do with your life? Chances are you're living a hit-or-miss, helter-skelter, shoot-from-the-hip life. Wouldn't you like a set of tools to help you realize your dreams and make sound, honest decisions that are true to your innermost self?

Then Inner Fitness is for you!

By practicing the Inner Fitness Program for several months, Mary H. was able to come to terms with her dilemma. She realized the necessity of breaking out of her rut and following her dream, no matter what the cost or how great the risk. She sent for college applications and read up on California. Then she decided to bring her children into the decision-making process. To her amazement, they understood and supported her. After much soul searching and discussion, her son Jay suggested a way for them all to pitch in. He and his sister would stay with their aunt until Mary was settled in California. Then, when they joined her, Jay would get a part-time job and Sue would take on baby-sitting assignments. If they all sacrificed together, they could make a go of it.

Mary felt relieved and confident. She is living in San Diego with her family, working part time for the forestry service and taking classes toward her degree. She is closer to her children than ever before. And although her life is hard, she now enjoys a sense of inner, spiritual joy that makes it all worth while.

Ralph B. wasn't as fortunate. Like so many others, he continues to ignore the needs and wants of his deepest self and is in danger of extinguishing the passion and fire in his life. Without the benefit of Inner Fitness, he persists in stagnating, wallowing in self-pity, convinced that he is trapped by circumstances beyond his control.

As Mary learned, achieving Inner Fitness is neither simple nor easy. It requires that we be open-minded, true to ourselves, and willing to make the effort to overcome our mental inertia. It can be painful and risky. Still, by practicing on our little problems, we will notice progress and improvement as soon as we begin working with the Tools for Living. When we make Inner Fitness, like physical fitness, a natural, daily part of our lives, we will find ourselves changing profoundly, from the inside out, and will be ready and eager to deal with that change. We will develop more positive and creative attitudes and have a deeper understanding of ourselves and others. Living life to its fullest, we will be ready to enjoy our future.

The Inner Fitness Program is designed as much for those of us who function well and enjoy life (but who want to function and live better) as for those of us who are unhappy. The program is also intended for those seeking advancement in business and careers as well as those of us desiring to enhance our personal lives. Because the skills we need for living well and for succeeding in business are one and the same, Inner Fitness will help us in all areas of our lives. In order to function at our peak in business, we must be in sync with ourselves and conditioned for optimum performance. By making us whole and by strengthening our decision-making powers, Inner Fitness aims to make us better managers and improve our overall productivity.

Open your mind and put on your emotional sweats. Together we will practice new ways of perceiving and communicating, so that we can achieve peak performance and develop a lasting state of Inner Harmony and Inner Fitness.

_t h r e e_

# INNER FITNESS:
# THE WARM-UP

**B**efore we begin our Inner Fitness workout and begin training with the Tools for Living, we must warm up our mental and emotional muscles by focusing briefly on the slippery roles that perception, language, and communication play in our lives. The first step in the Inner Fitness Program is the recognition that the bulk of our personal and business problems are traceable to difficulties with the way we perceive and communicate. By identifying and then breaking free of outmoded patterns of perceiving and communicating, we will escape from the emotional prison of the "I Should" life and into the creative freedom of the "I Choose" life.

## PERCEPTION: THE KEY

**Whether we are happy or sad, successful or unsuccessful, depends less on the world around us than on our perception of that world.**

Is the glass half empty or half full? The information we select and how we process that information to determine our perception and create meaning is a personal matter, conditioned by our personality, intelligence, and temperament. The facts we select in making a judgment or an evaluation are uniquely *"our* facts," not *"the* facts." That means we're not slaves to circumstance but are free to interpret the world in our own way.

Consider the case of Barry R., a young writer who worked for two years on his first novel, a techno-thriller. Filled with anxiety, he submits his manuscript to an agent. When the agent accepts it and agrees to represent him, he's delighted. And confident. A month later, however, when the first few rejection letters arrive, Barry is crushed. He takes the rejections personally, seeing them as evidence of his failings as a human being and as a writer. He falls into a deep depression, resolves to give up writing, and asks the agent not to submit the manuscript to any more houses.

But is that the only meaning of the rejection letters? Barry's interpretation of those letters depends on his own perception of himself and the world. In fact, two of the publishing houses rejected the manuscript simply because they already had techno-thrillers on their fall list. A third editor said it wasn't quite right for her, rejecting it because she didn't fall in love with the story or the main character. Barry didn't know about these reasons, but because of his own insecurity, he perceived a reality of the publishing business (one that had little or nothing to do with the quality of his manuscript) as a personal rejection and let that perception affect his whole life.

Perceptions can be based upon narrow, incomplete, or faulty evaluations or motivated by hidden causes and emotions. And these misperceptions can adversely affect our personal and professional lives and radically misshape or destroy our futures. As Dr. Terry Richards, a prominent New York psychologist, says, "Eighty percent of the problems of people in therapy can be traced to inaccurate or unrealistic perceptions."

**Only when we realize that *we* impose our own personal inter-**

pretation upon the world, will we be in a position to take control of our own lives. In order to do that, however, we must first learn to avoid the many pitfalls and traps that our very language sets up for us.

## LANGUAGE AND LABELS

I've seen the dangers of language over and over in my sales work. A middle-aged couple, believing that stocks are "risky" and that banks are "safe" and "secure," tuck their life's savings away in a low-yield savings bank, ignoring warnings about the inflationary spiral. Ten years later, to their dismay, they discover that inflation has eaten away at the buying power of their dollars and that they actually have lost rather than gained money as a result of their "safe" investment. Because of a label and a misconception, the couple jeopardized their financial security.

We all do it every day: assign easy labels to people and situations so we can fit them neatly into the cubbyholes of our minds. But this obsession with labeling and categorizing is a focal point of trouble. It makes a shambles of our perceptual process and a nightmare of our attempts at interpersonal communication.

WORDS, LANGUAGE, AND LABELS AREN'T JUST ACA-
DEMIC MATTERS. THE WAY WE USE THEM PRO-
FOUNDLY AFFECTS THE WAY WE PERCEIVE OUR-
SELVES AND THE WORLD.

The assumptions and implications of language are potent forces in
determining how we think, what we feel, the size of our bank ac-
counts, and the shape of our futures. Like parasites, these assumptions
get under our skin and infect us without our ever realizing it. They
make us jump to self-defeating conclusions and respond in narrow,
predetermined ways, leading us into lives of role playing. They create
treacherous verbal minefields that can destroy business deals and ruin
valued relationships.

> **Beware! The hidden assumptions of language can control our
> behavior and our lives.**

Some time ago, I attended a cocktail party on New York City's
Upper East Side. My host, who didn't know me very well, made the
mistake of introducing me as Victor Dishy, investment salesman. Keying on the word "sales," the guests backed away as if I were going to
charm the money out of their billfolds. They never bothered to ascertain that I actually was an investment counselor or that I wrote music
or had spent years studying and running workshops in communication
theory.

I've done the same kind of assuming. Introduced to a balding accountant, I accepted the stereotype that he was dull and conservative only to discover, to my surprise, that the man wrote poetry and played guitar in a rock 'n' roll band.

Labels are blinders that narrow our vision and restrict our understanding. Words loaded with prejudgments, predetermined meanings and values turn into labels. Consider words such as "communism" and "homosexual." Don't they transmit a host of highly charged connotations above and beyond their straightforward definition? That's because labels represent a way of thinking that views the world as fixed and rational, filled only with facts, clear-cut categories, and neat cubbyholes. When we confuse the particular with the general, when statements are made without qualifications, when we ignore the irrational, unpredictable human element and assume words apply the same way to all people under all circumstances for all purposes, then communication becomes an empty exchange of labels.

Because an ambitious young woman is labeled as a "secretary," her insightful opinions on corporate policy are ignored and she is overlooked for promotion to an executive position.

Because we label a relationship as "hopeless" (not stating a fact but describing a set of circumstances colored by our evaluation), we stop thinking creatively and abandon our efforts to salvage a once-rewarding bond.

Because we label ourselves as "lazy," we continue to stagnate, never bothering to ascertain the root causes of our own lack of productivity. Labeling is inherent in our language and promotes a narrow, close-minded view of the world. The aim of Inner Fitness, though, is to open our minds, reveal our options, and sharpen our mental and emotional skills. To do that, we must become aware of how we use labels (and how they use us). In so doing, we can gain mastery over our language and, consequently, over ourselves.

Of course, when properly used, labels and classifications are essential elements of our thought and communication processes. They enable us to grasp and simplify complex ideas, make intelligent calculations, and avoid needless repetition. But **when we indulge in inappropriate labeling not only of things but of people and human behavior, when we categorize and classify falsely and indiscriminately, then words become our masters rather than our tools.**

Our obsession with labels is indicative of a deeper, more pernicious problem. By assuming that everything in the world—thoughts, things, people—can be classified and categorized, we subscribe to an overly rational, mechanistic world view that squeezes out our humanity and devalues our feelings, our intuitions, our spirituality. Such a view confines us to a linear, stimulus-response pattern of thinking. It stunts our imagination and inhibits our creative potential.

What we must do is reconnect with our feelings, reawaken our creativity and reexperience the exhilaration of freedom of choice.

## COMMUNICATION: A PERSONAL MATTER

Miscommunication arises when we assume that words have universal meanings. But words are not objective carriers of information, nor is the communication process one in which the speaker and listener, sender and receiver, interpret the message in precisely the same way.

The message I send means something specific to me. I send it for a particular purpose and imbue it with my own feelings and connotations. You, the reader or listener, receive the message and respond to it within your own context of ideas, feelings, and purposes. The message does not read or sound or mean the same to the sender as to the receiver.

When, in proposing marriage, Bob C. tells Joan M. that he needs her and wants her, what he means by "need" and "want" and what she reads into those words may be totally different. So different, in fact, that their marriage falters when Joan discovers that Bob "needs" a housewife and mother rather than a companion and soulmate, as she imagined. (This example is pursued in more detail in Chapter 9, The Bow Tie).

Too often we assume that "my meaning is your meaning." But most words don't carry neutral, objective meaning; they're not innocent bystanders to our communication process. Words are charged with all sorts of connotations and moral and emotional implications.

Why? Because our efforts at communication are influenced and colored by an assemblage of prejudgments, habits, values, prejudices, and opinions—the accumulated baggage of our lives. No matter how hard we try, we can never remain pristinely objective. We impose our temperament, personality, experience, and intelligence on every sentence we hear, say, or write and on every situation we observe or in which we participate. Understanding this will help us master the art of communicating and put us on the road to breaking old habits and replacing them with new, more effective patterns.

**Only when we uncover, revise, and utilize the hidden influences on our language will we change our life from a hit-or-miss experience into a skillful, ever-developing adventure that will help us achieve Inner Fitness.**

Making fundamental changes in how we perceive and communicate is easier than it seems, because we're actually getting ourselves back in concert with nature rather than devising new behavior patterns. The Tools for Living will help us make that fundamental change in our lives. They will permit us to express our natural selves—that unique spirituality within each of us. Once we've freed ourselves of unhealthy response patterns, we will grow naturally into the best we can be.

Now that we've warmed up with some theoretical observations, it's time to get specific by jogging our emotions and stretching our minds on the mental-training circuit I call the Tools for Living. By reading about and practicing the six interrelated tools that follow, we will learn to educate our feelings, recondition our responses, and get in touch with our spiritual core, thereby triggering healthier, more effective behavior.

*p a r t*

2

THE TOOLS

FOR LIVING

# LIVING TOOL 1: THE DROP OF ELMER'S GLUE

Just think about how many people you know who talk endlessly about themselves, interrupting you to offer their opinions and advice but who have no interest in listening to what *you* have to say. How many times have you tried to tell someone about something—perhaps a new restaurant you'd discovered—only to be cut short with, "That's nothing. Let me tell you about the new restaurant *I* went to." Aren't we all guilty of that at times? Isn't it refreshing and enjoyable—and rare—when someone actually shuts up and *listens* to us, reacts, laughs at our jokes, and responds to us instead of being so preoccupied as to seem oblivious to our existence?

If only we could learn how to control the use of words so that they foster healthy interpersonal relations, help us heal rifts between friends and family, and lead us toward effective, productive communication. Achieving these goals simply and easily is the aim of our first Tool for Living.

## INTRODUCING LIVING TOOL 1: THE DROP OF ELMER'S GLUE

**What Elmer's Glue holds together even a champion bodybuilder cannot pull apart. Thus, a symbolic drop of epoxy glue, placed between the lips, represents the voluntary sealing of our mouths when we sense that we should be silent for a moment** (Fig. 1). The Drop of Glue means more than just be quiet; it reminds us to stop interfering, making assumptions, and jumping to conclusions.

Resisting the drive to rush into words isn't easy, and the more facile

FIGURE I. ELMER'S GLUE

we are at words, the more difficult it becomes. Just as we have the power to open our mouths and talk, though, so we have the power to turn off those words. Hear yourself filling the air with words and imagine that you are placing a *real* drop of epoxy glue between your lips. Although your vocal cords may strain and your eyes bulge, given sufficient imagination on your part, you will not speak.

When do we use this first Tool for Living?

When we are about to make an important decision. When we have to choose what action to take. When we are responding to our environment in a serious way. When we are engaged in a conversation or negotiation that is not going right. When we catch ourselves latching on to one little piece of information, one word or one action, and giving it far more importance than it deserves. Anytime, in fact, that we sense that we are in danger of falling into a bad habit or about to rely on our battery of stereotyped responses instead of seeking out a fresh, more appropriate response.

Use the Drop of Elmer's Glue and many healthful results will follow. We will no longer jump to unwarranted conclusions. We will hold ourselves back from irrational thinking. We won't rush to label and pigeonhole people and events. We will restrain our critical, judgmental selves. We will become better listeners and, consequently, better, more confident communicators because we will be able to focus our attention on another human being. And that means eliminating the need to rush into words and maintain conscious control of the moment. By listening instead of talking, learning to absorb information with not only our ears but with all of our senses, we will perceive more of the world around us. Consequently, we will expand our base of information. Being more attuned to others will make us more adept at communicating with them "on their own wavelengths." In this way, we can sidestep many of the unhealthy conflicts and frictions caused by misunderstanding and miscommunicating with those around us.

Remaining silent allows our perception-processing machinery time to consider whether or not we have all the pertinent facts. It allows us to determine whether the meaning and significance we are about to attribute to a situation is valid, whether an action we are about to take is wise, and whether we are on the right track in our approach.

Why? Because the Drop of Elmer's Glue contains one simple, blockbuster message that could change your life. It reminds you, above all, to:

## Delay your responses

By adhering to this simple message—delaying your responses for a second, a minute, an hour, or even a month—you will short-circuit the hubbub of words and plug yourself back into the moment. Instead of simply reacting to the world, you will begin to stop, look, and act smart. The Drop of Elmer's Glue is truly the "pause that refreshes," because it allows you to start from scratch and take control of your actions and, thus, your life.

Try it now. Don't react immediately to my statement. Don't accept it, don't dismiss it, don't argue with it. Concentrate on the idea of the delayed response. Then pause. Delay. Let it sink in. Roll it around in your brain. Is there more here than you initially thought? Think of the last time you lost your temper. What would have happened if you had simply delayed your response instead of blowing up on the spot? Think of the last time you acted obsessively or compulsively. Would you have acted the same way if you had held yourself back from reacting immediately? Think of the last major decision you made. Would a delayed response have led you to a different conclusion?

What happens in a crisis when we don't think we have the time to delay our responses or when we have to make an immediate decision in order to gain an advantage? That is precisely the moment when a delay is most needed. The more hectic and pressured the situation, the calmer we must become. Because our minds work at lightning speed, the delay need only be a fraction of a second. That pause, however, can be enough for us to cut our internal circuitry and absorb the situation, evaluate our options, and make a more appropriate, more creative decision. The more we practice delaying our responses, the shorter that delay time will become.

## ELMER'S GLUE CAN CHANGE YOUR LIFE

An employer who talks so much that she never listens to the ideas of her employees. A young woman who is so meek and fearful that she is afraid to leave the house. A man who is so oversensitive and quick to take offense that he can't hold a job. A husband who is so jealous that he imagines his wife is having an affair with every man she talks to. All of these people could use a Drop of Elmer's Glue.

*Most neurotic behavior would be eliminated if only we learned to use Elmer's Glue and delay our reactions.* Delaying responses isn't going to eliminate all neurotic patterns overnight, but it certainly will attack the core of the problem, rigidity. Elmer's Glue, though, will do more than help us overcome our personal hang-ups; it will be of direct benefit in our business careers.

An employee whom I'd fired returned asking for reinstatement. Just as I was about to say, "I'm sorry, there's nothing I can do and, anyway, it's against company policy to rehire you," I remembered the Drop of Elmer's Glue. I paused for what must have been no more than a second. Recalling the minor incident that had prompted his firing, I recognized, sheepishly, that I had been wrong. I'd been in a foul mood and had made a big deal out of a little event. Turning to the young man, I said, "Well what are you waiting for? Take off your coat and get to work." That young man turned into one of my best salesmen.

Of course, there were times I didn't delay my response and paid the price. A pre-law student, Diane K., was working for me as an administrative assistant. When she asked for more responsibility and a fifty-percent pay increase, I summarily turned down her request, and she quit. I was thinking only of my salary caps and may have been influenced by a touch of male chauvinism. Had I used Elmer's Glue, I would have realized not only that Diane deserved the promotion but that handing over additional job responsibilities to her would free me to pursue other ventures and actually allow me to increase my income. Diane became a successful lawyer, and I had a great deal of trouble replacing her. I hate to think of how much that missing Drop of Glue cost me in dollars, hours, and anxiety.

Consider another example. At one point in my career I was the sales manager of a large real estate syndication firm. The firm sent out information booklets to potential customers who had responded to a direct-mail inquiry. When I sat down to compose the covering letter to accompany the booklet, I was at a loss. The prospective client had already received one letter and was about to receive a booklet. What more was there to say? Instead of repeating the message yet again, I applied a Drop of Elmer's Glue and paused. Almost without realizing what I was doing, I folded a sheet of paper into quarters and attached it to the booklet with a paper clip. On the outside quarter I wrote, "Thank you for your inquiry," and on the inside I introduced an account executive and invited the client to visit our offices. The hard, businesslike quality of a cover letter was softened into a visually warm, attractive, and personal note. Without thinking in words, I realized that a cover letter didn't have to be a letter. Thanks to Elmer's Glue, the results were outstanding.

Delaying our responses develops a receptivity to creative thinking. Instead of leaping to compare a new situation with previous ones, we become more attuned to searching out what is different, even unique.

> **Look for the differences: even a small one can make a big change in your life.**

# A  D E E P E R  S P I R I T U A L
# S I L E N C E

In order to get in touch with our true selves and live the "I Choose" life, there are times when we must respond to our environment on a nonverbal level. We sense and feel but do not yet rush to convert sensations into articulated words and labels. Just as the rhythm and timing of dancers and athletes are derived, in part, from their ability to control their breathing, so can our inner rhythm and timing be traced to our ability to attain silence. Pure silence opens the pores of our senses. It allows us to drink in what each new day has to offer and to perceive with our whole being. *Pure silence is the unhurried breathing in with our senses and the pause we engage in before we breathe out with words and thoughts.*

| An empty mind is the beginning of wisdom. |
| --- |

Unfortunately, there are many barriers preventing us from attaining inner silence. In addition to our passion for verbalization and the Western world's love affair with words, there is the fear silence engenders. We clutch at words as a tool to help explain the unfamiliar. Silence, however, tears us away from the safe, the known, the predictable, away from the assumed stability of the "I Should" life. It threatens to open us up to new ways of thinking and feeling that challenge our current opinions. Silence forces us to sublimate our talkiness and our egos and forego control over ourselves and others. For many of us, such a prospect is scary; it's far easier to talk about cutting loose from words than actually doing it. And yet, we must find ways of bringing more pure silence into our lives.

Feel free to use any technique that works best in order to help you achieve deep inner silence: meditation, training in sensory awareness—any program that works for you. **The more in touch we are with our verbal-free selves, the more rewarding and creative our ultimate decisions and actions will be, and the more joy we will experience.**

Of course, inner silence alone is not enough. The goal of Inner Fitness is to meld spirituality, dreams, and action in a synergistic marriage, which I call, "Applied Spirituality." Just as pure rationalism without spirituality is unproductive and unsatisfying, attaining deep silence is not enough without the establishment and fulfillment of conscious goals. Elmer's Glue, therefore, is but one in a series of six Tools for Living.

In order to develop the skill of using Elmer's Glue, we must practice applying it to our lives on a daily basis. To help us, I offer the following Conditioning Exercises.

# TOOLS FOR LIVING
# CONDITIONING EXERCISES:
# THE DROP OF ELMER'S GLUE

## Step 1: Using Elmer's Glue—Delay Your Responses

1. *Use the Tool.* Hold a real tube or bottle of glue in your hands. Read the label. Imagine that in addition to binding paper, wood, and plastic, the glue can seal your lips together. Carry the tube around for one day to remind you to practice silence and delay your responses.

2. *Stop a destructive habit.* No matter how hard it may be to admit, all of us have some disruptive or neurotic habit patterns. Pick out one of yours. Maybe you're always late for appointments or you continually misplace your keys or you eat compulsively. The next time you're about to fall into that pattern, apply a Drop of Elmer's Glue and delay your action. Get silent. Note if the delayed response brings about any change at all in the way you act. Try this with different habit patterns you would like to change.

3. *Listen.* The next time you're about to interrupt someone, stop, apply a Drop of Elmer's Glue, and listen instead. Concentrate on what that person is saying to you. Make an effort to understand that person's point of view instead of jumping in to express your own. Do this and you will find that your listening skills and, consequently, your communication skills, will improve dramatically. You

may very well make new friends and achieve greater success in your business.

4. *Control your temper.* The next time you feel yourself getting angry and about to lose your temper, apply a Drop of Elmer's Glue to your lips and delay your reaction. Take a deep breath. Wait. Ask yourself what the consequences of your anger will be. Is there a good reason for your anger, or are you simply venting your own frustration? Pausing may dissipate some of your anger and will help you to avoid unnecessary aggravation.

5. *Control runaway thinking.* Use Elmer's Glue to control irrational, out-of-control thinking. Prevent yourself from creating problems where none exist. For example, you're waiting for someone you care about to call. A half hour goes by. You start thinking he or she won't call. You start imagining why. The person's injured, doesn't love you, or has found something better to do. Stop! Apply Elmer's. Don't let this kind of runaway thinking undermine your self-image. Recognize that you have the power to stop your mind from drawing unwarranted conclusions.

6. *Don't jump to conclusions.* On the basis of one brief meeting, you're about to conclude that you don't like someone. Apply Elmer's Glue. Suspend your judgment. Avoid stereotyping. Look for this person's unique characteristics, and give him or her another chance.

7. *Review your turning points.* Pick out and review one of the key turning points in your life. What if you had paused before making that key decision and stripped your mind of words and preconcep-

tions? Would you have acted differently? Use Elmer's to help you analyze and reevaluate that decision and to help you make your *next* major decision.

## Step 2: Practicing Inner Silence

1. *Stare at a word.* Write down a word on a piece of paper in big capital letters. Now stare at that word continuously, concentrating on each letter until it begins to lose its meaning and becomes a jumble of letters. Or pick a word and repeat it aloud over and over until it begins to sound strange and empty of meaning. By breaking the hold of words on our minds and shattering their reality, we will open and stimulate our senses and put ourselves in closer touch with our instincts and inner self.

2. *Visualize.* Lie down on the floor and close your eyes. Take a deep breath and, as you exhale, relax each part of your body—head, neck, lower back, pelvis, thighs, calves, ankles—until you feel the contact of your flesh against the ground. Visualize your body as the floor would see it, as if you were looking up from beneath the ground. Concentrate on that visual image of yourself in order to help you suppress your words.

3. *Become an infant again.* Using deep breathing, yoga, meditation, Zen, or whatever technique appeals to you, practice getting in closer touch with your inner self and hearing the sound of inner silence. Try to imagine how, as an infant, you reacted to the world around you.

4. *Face the challenge of an empty piece of paper.* Using pen, pencil, or watercolors, draw whatever *you* want, concentrating on drawing only what pleases you without considering what you think you *should* be drawing. Suspend your aesthetic judgment. Don't consider whether your creation is beautiful or ugly, whether anyone else would or would not like it. Can you do it? If not, clear your mind and try again. The ability to suspend judgment is an important part of Inner Fitness.

5. *Sense without labeling.* Set aside five minutes each day to concentrate on sensing without labeling. Wherever you are, close your eyes and pick up some object in front of you. Don't name it, just feel it. Notice its shape, its texture. Smell it. Shake it and listen to it. Touch it to your lips. Rub it against your skin. Then open your eyes. Aren't you now seeing this object in a fresh, new light? Isn't it relaxing not to pour all your energies into words and analysis? Sensing without labeling will help us excite our creativity.

6. *Use your imagination.* This time, instead of actually grasping an object, close your eyes and just imagine one. Let's start with a cookie. Imagine you're holding it in your hand, about to eat it. What kind of cookie is it? Visualize its texture and the way it crumbles in your hand. Imagine you're putting the cookie in your mouth. How does it smell and taste? Are you dropping crumbs into your lap? Repeat this exercise every few days to help you develop your imagination and enhance your verbal-free thinking.

7. *Feel.* Next time you walk down the street, make an effort to *feel* yourself touch the ground. Are you stepping lightly? Is your toe or your heel hitting the ground first? What does this tell you about the

way you feel today? The more in touch we become with our feelings and sensations, the more control we will have over them and the more they will provide a fertile, healthy soil for productive decisions.

_f i v e_

# LIVING TOOL 2:
# THE BELLS

I remember one summer, when I was no more than ten, running down the street toward the ball field in the small town in which we spent our vacations. My Louisville Slugger is slung over my shoulder, my glove hooked over my bat. I'm running like the wind.

Suddenly, I hear the roar of an approaching train in the distance. Its shrill whistle bursts the summer silence. Just as I reach the railroad crossing, the bells ring out, the red lights flash, and the gates descend. I jump up and down impatiently. Darn! I'm stuck on the wrong side of the tracks. I'm going to have to wait!

I tiptoe toward the rails and look down at the speeding face of the approaching locomotive. Although bursting to fly across, certain I can make it, I hear those bells ringing in my ears and remember my mother's warning to "Stop, look, and listen before crossing." Her words in my ears, I picture myself tripping and falling as I try to sprint across the railroad tracks. I hear the frantic whistle and the screech of breaks, imagine the train rolling over me and my mother's horror-struck face.

Needless to say, I stood still, shaking in my sneakers, and watched the train fly by. The engineer waved to me. The danger passed and my afternoon of baseball was all the sweeter because I heeded the warning signs.

That childhood image has stuck with me through life. Countless crucial choices, emotional as well as rational, confront us as we grow up and proceed through life—but who or what is there to warn us? Wouldn't life be easier and more fulfilling if there were bells like those at the railroad crossing to alert us to the dangers of acting against our natures, of making unhealthy, unwise decisions, or of succumbing to destructive emotions?

Well, here they are!

## INTRODUCING
## LIVING TOOL 2:
## THE BELLS

**The Bells (Fig. 2) are a visual symbol representing the inner signals that we send to ourselves, the sensory messages warning us that we are in impending emotional danger or on the verge of making a serious error in judgment.**

FIGURE 2. THE BELLS

The function of the Bells is to alert us to oncoming dangers, whether small or large, personal or professional. When there is internal conflict, the Bells ring. They are the sounds one's will makes as it tries to express and preserve itself in a hostile environment. When we learn to identify and respond to our internal Bells, we will learn to avoid the dangerous but often subtle emotional pitfalls that stand in the way of our inner fitness.

## THE SOUND OF THE BELLS

What are inner signals and how do we recognize them?

Each person has his or her own set of unique warning signs. Often they are physical. For me, it's a tightening of my neck and shoulder muscles. For my wife, Zaida, it's a cramping, churning stomach. Maybe you get a pounding headache. Or your lower back aches. Or you get hives. You grind your teeth. Your palms sweat. Your leg shakes. You can't make eye contact. You crave a cigarette or a beer.

Maybe your Bells don't ring out in a straightforward physical way. Maybe you feel vaguely irritable or lose your temper easily. Or you feel tense and uptight or struggle with doubts, worries, and free-floating hostility. Whatever it may be, each of us has his or her own internal way of saying, "Watch out!" "Be Careful!" "Uh oh!"

These signals are the silent voices of our inner selves calling out to us when we're procrastinating or shirking an important task. Or when we're about to plunge into a self-destructive act, fail to speak up or react in the face of mistreatment, rush into an ill-conceived judgment, or commit a blunder. There are signals anytime we're about to do something that we know, deep down, is wrong for us, anytime that we're not getting the most out of life.

Many of us downgrade or even ignore our feelings and intuitions. No matter how hard we try to arrange our lives into rational packages, however, our intuitive, "softer side" always manages to undo the wrapping. I say, "Good, let it." The Bells exemplify the best of that "softer" inner self. They help us regain access to our true natures by leading us to unblock our channels, break old thinking habits, and clear a path for self-expression. **Only by listening to and acting on our intuitions will we be able to fuse thinking and feeling and learn to respond as a whole person.**

Unfortunately, many of us don't hear our Bells. Because we've lost touch with our feelings, values, and desires, we soundproof ourselves against the sound of our Bells. We cushion ourselves with rationalizations, fantasies, busy work, anything we can think of to keep us from hearing the inner warnings that might put us in touch with our feelings and make us look at ourselves with a fresh, new perspective. Or we become so dismissive of our instincts and inner signals that we learn to block them out as if they were nothing but annoying background noise. The task of our second Living Tool is to help put us back in touch with, *and* act on, these inner warning signs.

For those of us whose lives are full of anxiety, pressures, and sensory overload, our Bells may ring so constantly that we learn to ignore them and block them from our minds. With dangers lurking everywhere, we may find it impossible to distinguish one Bell from another. If that's the case, don't fret. Learning to interpret the Bells takes practice and, later in the chapter, I offer advice on how to become more adept in understanding the differences among the Bells. Meanwhile, remember that the Bells ring when we are about to act against our *innermost* selves not when we are faced with *external* crises over which we have no control. Consequently, every emergency, every anxiety attack, every problem that demands immediate attention, need not start our Bells ringing.

June B. is standing patiently in line at the supermarket. While thumbing through *People* magazine, a woman with a large basket of food cuts in front of her. June fumes with anger. Her stomach tightens. She curses under her breath. Her Bells are ringing out. Although she's dying to speak up, she convinces herself that it doesn't matter; that it's not worth making a fuss about. But her heart is pounding in rage. When she gets home, she's so worked up that she drops the groceries, breaks two bottles of soda, and snaps at her son. If only she'd told that pushy woman to get back in line. . . .

Richard D. and Anne K. are contemplating marriage. They've been dating for six months, like each other's company, and share many interests. Their only problem is sex—it's been awkward and unsatisfying. Anne has been living on her own since she was eighteen and has had several long-term relationships. But Richard comes from a strict, religious background and has had only limited sexual experience. Anne becomes tense every time she thinks about Richard's awkward and unsatisfying lovemaking. Because she loves him, she believes that their sexual problems will disappear after they've spent more time together. Ignoring her Bells—the warning that their sexual problem may be indicative of a far deeper problem—she marries Richard. The sex does not improve. Other tensions arise. The marriage lasts less than a year. If only she had heeded her warning Bells. . . .

Lisa C. works as a designer in the garment district. She is a tall, attractive brunette, single, living in a studio apartment on Manhattan's Upper West Side. She would love to have a bigger apartment, would love to buy a fur coat, would love to send more money to her mother in Topeka. Unfortunately, she can't afford to. Although she's taken on more and more job responsibility in the past year, her salary is still meager and she hasn't received an increase in over a year and a half. She knows she deserves a raise, but she dreads asking, feeling she shouldn't have to beg. What if she's turned down? She doesn't want to look for another job. She likes her fellow workers, the company, her office. Lisa has soundproofed herself so well that she's muffled the sound of her Bells. So she just goes on working, worrying, and scraping by, torn up inside, while her boss sits back patiently, perfectly satisfied to have her slave away for him at a pittance. If only she'd spoken up, opened her ears and her heart to the message of those Bells. . . .

What about your own Bells?

Do you have a volatile temper? Aren't there warning signs that tell you when you're about to explode?

Do you have an employee who comes in late, leaves early, and never seems to be around when you need him? Do you ignore the obvious signs of his incompetence because you don't want to take on the unpleasant task of firing him?

Are you holding on to a stock that's dropped ten points in the last week? Are you ignoring the advice of your broker, your spouse, and your inner Bells because you're hard up for cash and hope against hope that the stock will bounce back?

Are you suddenly stumbling over things, cutting your finger, bumping into furniture? Isn't your body trying to tell you something?

All of us have inner warning signals. A major step toward Inner Fitness is conditioning ourselves to pick up the cues coming from our bodies and to hear those Bells loud and clear.

"Sure, sure, I hear Bells," you might say. "Big deal. That doesn't mean I can do anything about them. Everybody wishes they could act on their gut feelings, but who does?"

You're right, of course. Simply hearing Bells is not nearly enough. Just as a sales representative who doesn't come back with a check is merely a conversationalist, so we become mere bystanders to our lives when we hear but fail to act on our inner signals. To sell ourselves on Inner Fitness, therefore, we have to *heed* the warnings of the Bells and condition ourselves to *act* accordingly. Why? Because every time our Bells ring, we face a moment of truth. Their clanging compels us to ask a critical question: Do I believe in myself enough to act on my instincts?

We have been brainwashed from childhood not to trust our instincts. We are expected to be able to present a purely logical, rational case for any contemplated action. Acting on "just a feeling" or a whim will not raise our "maturity" or intelligence rating. And yet our healthy inner signals, while they cannot always be defended with cold rationality, are wise enough to alert us to potential troubling situations. They guide us into taking calculated risks and into dealing with probabilities.

From the moment of birth we face a battle of wills that lasts a lifetime. When we succumb and dedicate our lives to conformity, adapting, and living the "I Should" life, we rob ourselves of the emotional strength necessary to act on our instincts. We turn passivity into a virtue. Building our emotional muscles and regenerating our belief in ourselves is what we should be doing—not because anyone tells us we should but because it is in our own best interest.

## THE KEY TO THE BELLS: KNOWING IS NOT ENOUGH

The human body already has a built-in reflex system that allows us to avoid physical dangers. When our hands touch fire, we draw back automatically, without thinking. When someone kicks at our loins, we instinctively protect them with our hands. When a car swerves toward us, we jump out of the way. Our natural defense mechanism works as a single, conditioned response for our self-preservation.

The threat of physical danger triggers us to action, yet we persist in ignoring threats to our emotional and mental well-being. To rectify that and develop Inner Fitness, we need an Early Warning System that alerts us to the debilitating stresses and emotional traps of modern life —the stifling tensions and unfulfilled desires that threaten our relationships, our careers, our personal lives. These stumbling blocks prevent us from living a full, creative life.

The Bells, our second Tool for Living, is just that warning system.

They are part of our intricate inner communication network that tells us when to avoid danger, when to sleep and eat, when we need a vacation, when we've had too much or not enough.

## UNCOVERING THE HIDDEN POWER OF THE BELLS

What is the secret that turns a vague, visceral feeling into a reliable habit pattern?

The secret is recognizing that:

> **Ignoring your bells is life-threatening.**

That may sound like an exaggeration, but it's not. Think of the Bells as a surgeon general's warning implanted in our brains.

If we *don't* act on our Bells, we internalize our anger and frustration and make ourselves sick with substitutes for action—anxiety, stress, or depression—and risk mental and physical illness. We blame ourselves. We mope. We become cranky. We become trapped in the quicksand of the "I Should" life. The message of the Bells rings out clearly: act now or suffer later.

If we don't act on the internal, nonverbal signs that warn us of dangers in our jobs, our investments, and our relationships, we will undermine both the length and quality of our lives. If we pay no heed to the voices that call out our craving for artistic expression or job satisfaction, we will be sentencing ourselves to a boring, painful life in which we squander our energy and creative potential.

Only when we feel in our guts that *the mistakes we make as a result of refusing to acknowledge and obey our inner signals are as life-threatening as any purely physical threats,* will we be compelled to act. Our natural drive for self-preservation won't allow us to stand by passively.

Why? Because responding to the Bells taps into our existing, built-in self-preservation mechanism, commonly referred to as "fight or flight."

An emotional malfunction presents a real and life-threatening danger. Visualize what will happen to us down the road if we stay in an unhappy job, continue an unhappy relationship, endure an unhappy life. The more vividly we visualize the damaging results of *not* listening to our Bells, the more our fear of *not* acting will outweigh our fear of acting. Conceive of what will happen if we yield to that high-pressure salesman and buy what we don't want or when we're not ready. Or if we allow the first signs of bickering with our lover to go unconfronted.

I'm not advocating that you rush out and follow every passing urge that pops into your head. Instincts must be evaluated properly (even though it's my opinion that, were we forced to choose, we would learn more and be wiser following our every whim than fearfully sidestepping every risk). Sometimes, in order to save our souls, we may even choose to accept risks to our lives in order to stand up for our principles. What I *am* advocating, however, is that we believe in the medical and emotional necessity of acting wisely on those instincts.

## TURNING THE BELLS INTO A LIVING SKILL

How do you learn to turn these Bells into a skill for living?

**By practicing daily.**

We've all heard the expression that there are only two things certain in life: death and taxes. Well I think there's a third: it's certain that every day will bring its share of friction. Without fail, someone or something will irritate or upset us. Let's enlist these daily irritations in the cause of toughening our emotional resolve.

I call these bits of friction the Little Bells. Acting on them is generally easy enough, requiring a touch of self-assertion and a little effort of will but no deep emotional commitment. The consequences are small and manageable.

You open the mail and read the plumber's bill: five hundred dollars! That's fifty dollars more than the estimate. Don't stew about it. Call the plumber. Speak up. Express your indignation. Refuse to pay the additional amount.

A taxi driver is rude to you. Tell him so. Get it off your chest.

You're seated at a restaurant. A woman at the next table is smoking and you're allergic to cigarettes. Ask her to put out her cigarette. Or ask to be moved to a different table. Take some small, positive action!

You've been putting off calling your mother for weeks. Don't put it off any longer. Call her. You'll feel better. You'll free your mind.

You've negotiated for a new job and think all the details have been worked out. When you receive your contract, however, you discover the job title is "Manager" rather than "Director" as you'd expected. Don't stew. Don't say it doesn't matter. Ask for clarification. Ask for a change.

Little Bells may also ring when we feel the irritation and conflict caused by squelching a spontaneous urge.

You wake up and just don't feel like going to work. Although you know it'll be a slow day and that you won't really be missed, you don't feel right about calling in sick. Your Little Bells ring. Treat yourself to a holiday. Take a fling! Call in sick. Enjoy your freedom. In the long run, it will help your mental health *and* your productivity.

You see a beautiful pair of earrings in a store window. They match your new fall outfit perfectly. You can't really afford them; they're outside your budget. Your Little Bells ring. Go ahead and buy them anyway! Treat yourself. They'll help your self-image and your self-confidence. Find someplace else to cut back.

Conditioning ourselves to respond quickly and forcefully to our Little Bells, we will clear a behavioral path that will prove increasingly easy to follow in the future. Each time we act on our Bells, we make it easier to act the next time. Each time we ignore our Bells, we move closer to a breakdown in our natural response system and sink deeper and deeper into the quagmire of the "I Should" life. Conditioning ourselves to act increases our personal integrity and control of our own lives. Nothing, not even money, is sweeter than self-respect.

## TUNING IN TO THE TYPES OF BELLS

Bells have different sounds. The booming clang of giant Bells heralds the possibility of making serious mistakes in our lives. The tinkle of Little Bells signal the minor irritations that pop up on a daily basis. There are as many types of Bells as there are people. Becoming aware of the different types of Bells alerts us to hear and understand the true sound of our own Bells. From my experience talking to hundreds of people, and conducting Inner Fitness workshops, I have isolated a few of the most widely heard. These are alarms warning us of pernicious circumstances that require action. Recognizing and acting on these few Bells will put us well on our way to mastering this second Tool for Living.

## 1. The Sixth Sense Bells

The Sixth Sense Bells work below the surface of conscious, rational thought. They ring when we have a bad or good "feeling" about something or someone, even though we can't explain that feeling or express it in words. We meet someone for the first time to whom we take an instant dislike. We see a picture of a house and fall in love with it. We interview for a job that pays less than our current job but somehow feels more right for us. These feelings or instincts, coming from deep within us, are often more authentic, more salutary, than the responses of our conscious minds. If something "feels" wrong or right, we should listen to our sixth sense and go with that feeling.

Our intuition, after all, is an educated feeling. It does not spring from out of nowhere. It is based upon a computerlike evaluation of our past experiences and a spontaneous "brainstorming session" that takes place within us, enlisting all of our intellectual powers.

Acting on our Bells does not mean that we must act impetuously, nor does it disavow totally any need to analyze the positive action we are about to take. The danger lies in allowing an analysis to create a rationalization for inaction.

## 2. The Head-in-the-Sand Bells

The Head-in-the-Sand Bells ring every time we try to deny reality, duck our obligations, or avoid our responsibilities. Think of Anne K.'s denial of her sexual problem with Richard D. Imagine the actress who tries to skim over that one seemingly incongruous line when that very line may hold the key to creating her character believably and powerfully.

## 3. The Unfinished Business Bells

The Unfinished Business Bells ring when we put off doing what, deep down, we really want to do. Think of the person who yearns to play the guitar but never translates that yearning into action, the man who wants to begin a relationship with a woman he finds interesting and attractive but who is too timid to call her up and ask her out.

## 4. The "I'm Trapped" Bells

The "I'm Trapped" Bells ring when we feel physically and emotionally caged. Remember Ralph B., the advertising executive, and Mary H., the Boston mother, in Chapter 2, who were trapped by the limitations of their perceptions. These Bells remind us to take some action, any action, and that the most dangerous response to feeling trapped is to do nothing.

## 5. The Outside Forces Bells

The Outside Forces Bells warn us not to trust others blindly but to come to our own conclusions. These Bells advise us not to be intimidated by the confidence or arrogance of so-called experts. These Bells advise us not to let outside authority figures (be they parents, doctors, lawyers, or peers) make our decisions for us. They urge us to stand up for ourselves and not allow ourselves to be taken advantage of.

Your parents are pressuring you to go to college. You want an education but know you're not ready. Your Outside Forces Bells ring.

You're at a party. Someone offers you cocaine. You don't want it but your friends urge it on you. You listen to your Bells and resist.

## 6. The Personal Weakness Bells

Each of us has a weakness, a special bad habit, an Achilles heel. Some of us can't say, "No." Some are too quick to anger. Some are too pushy or too cowering. Others are lazy. Whenever your personal behavior problem is about to flare up, listen for your Personal Weakness Bells and consciously repress the drive to respond out of habit.

## 7. The Personal Ethics Bells

When we are about to lie or steal or cheat, or violate our moral imperative, we feel a twinge of conscience. This is the sound of our Personal Ethics Bells. Ignoring these bells may bring us short-term gains, but the long-term loss to ourselves is immeasurable. Some of us have learned to muffle these Bells. When we muffle the Personal Ethics Bells, however, we are being dishonest with ourselves and injurious to our inner spiritual core. For being so self-destructive, we will eventually pay the price in increased physical and mental anxiety.

## 8. The Semantic Bells

Our Semantic Bells ring when we run into conflict over the meaning or interpretation of a word. Words can be dangerous because they can lead us to confuse the general with the specific and thereby gloss over details, ignore subtleties and relationships, and close our eyes to the real world.

Heather W.'s dream was to help people, so she decided to become a nurse. Unfortunately, "nursing" was a generalization that told Heather little about the actual experience of nursing—the tedious work, the intense pressure, the grueling and irregular hours, the unbearable pettiness of the hospital bureaucracy, and the callous lack of respect from doctors and patients alike. Had Heather's Semantic Bells been working, she might not have confused "nursing" with being a nurse. Instead, she would have put a Drop of Elmer's Glue on her lips, paused, and focused on the reality of nursing rather than on talk about her dream of becoming a nurse. She would have spent a summer as a hospital volunteer, gathering firsthand experience, before she committed herself to nursing as a lifetime profession. Then she could have had a solid base for understanding and intelligent decision making.

If your Bells aren't working properly, don't worry. They're merely muffled from years of neglect. Of course, we won't change over night; it takes time and effort. But just as exercise and proper nutrition can help bring back our physical well-being, so conditioning with the Tools will put us back in touch with our instincts and tone our minds and emotions. And that's where the Conditioning Exercises come in.

## TOOLS FOR LIVING CONDITIONING EXERCISES: THE BELLS

### Step 1: Hearing Your Bells

1. *Listen for the Bells.*   How do they appear to you? As a hollow feeling in your gut? A tightening of the neck muscles? A weight pressing on your shoulders? A general feeling of discomfort or anxiety? Write down how your feelings of emotional stress and conflict manifest themselves. Next time you feel that way, stop yourself. Remember, our bodies talk to us: learn to listen.

2. *Ask a friend.*   If you're having trouble hearing your Bells, ask your spouse or a close friend if you exhibit any idiosyncrasies at moments of stress and what they are. The words of someone close to you may jog your mind and help you recognize your own triggers.

## Step 2: Pinpointing Your Bells

1. *Review the list of common Bells.* Pinpoint which present the most problems for you. Rate yourself on a scale of 1 to 10 on your ability to respond effectively to each of those Bells.

2. *List the Personal Weakness Bells (no. 6) that are of special relevance to you.* Do you have a special problem area, a hang-up, some situation that always creates conflict in you? Give each of your individual Bells a catchy title: for example, the "I Can't Take Criticism" Bells, the "I've Got a Chip on My Shoulder" Bells, or the "I'm Too Shy" Bells.

## Step 3: Acting on Your Bells

1. *Practice acting on your Little Bells.* Starting today, and every day for the next week, do one little thing that you've wanted to do for a long time. Speak up one time. Give in to one whim. Confront a minor irritation instead of allowing it to pass by and leave you frustrated. Take a little risk. Expand yourself. See how it feels.

2. *Recognize and act on your Sixth Sense Bells (no. 1).* Act on a feeling without bothering to analyze it. Follow your nose. You'll be surprised where it may lead you!

3. *Act on a different Bell every day.* Focus on each Bell for one full day. If you're shy, practice speaking up. If you're avoiding some small unpleasant task, go ahead and do it. If you're bored at work, take on a new task. Move to another Bell. Focus on *it* for one day. Do anything to get yourself in the habit of acting on your inner signals.

4. *Break a pattern.* Let's suppose you have free time tonight or tomorrow. Instead of watching television, force yourself to begin a task that you've been wanting to do but putting off for a long time. Write a letter, read a book, begin a project, go to a play. Been dreaming about being a writer? Stop dreaming. Write a thousand words today! Have you always wanted to be an actress? Stop wanting. Sign up for an acting class. Listen to your inner self. Don't put it off. Not listening is tantamount to committing passive psychological suicide. Conditioning yourself to act puts you on the road toward Inner Fitness and the "I Choose" life.

5. *Look back at the Bells you have ignored.* Was there one important time you acted against your nature or your better judgment? What signals did you ignore? If you had to do it over again, how would you have acted? How might your life be different today if you *had* acted? Use both the Bells and Elmer's Glue to help you analyze a past decision. The next time you hear the sound of your Bells, but are about to ignore them, apply Elmer's Glue. Pause. Stop rationalizing. Decide again if you want to ignore your inner signals.

6. *Face the present.*   Consider a troublesome situation you are now in. What will happen if you take action? What will happen if you take *no* action? How will you feel about yourself if you do or say nothing? *Visualize* the results of not listening to your Bells.

## LIVING TOOL 3:
## THE CIRCLE
## AND DOT

Shopping at Paul Stuart, an elegant men's store on Madison Avenue in New York City, used to give me fits. Once a year, I would decide to invest in a well-made suit and try to choose one from its vast selection. I kept trying on one suit after another. What a dilemma! What was my problem? What was I looking for?

In fact, I knew. I was looking for that one perfect suit to jump out at me and scream, "I'm the one!" Since that was not likely to happen and lacking the funds to buy all the suits, I couldn't make up my mind. The more I studied the rack of suits, the less appealing the choices became, and the emptier the racks seemed to grow. I was beginning to think there was really nothing to buy. Still, I kept on staring and considering, until the salesman lost all patience, plucked a pinstripe from the group, and said most determinedly, "This is the right suit for you, sir." Intimidated by the exasperation in his voice, I sheepishly accepted his decision. But even as I was paying for the suit, I was furtively eyeing a customer in a handsome English tattersall, thinking it was even more right for me than the pinstripe.

That's human nature, we say. We search for that one perfect solution, can't make up our minds, and then let someone else make the decision for us—and never really are happy with *that* decision. Or, trapped by circumstance, we narrow our vision and refuse to see any acceptable options at all. We look at a rack full of choices and see nothing. Either way, we avoid the anxiety of accepting full responsibility and shut our minds to opportunity.

But that's *not* human nature and that's *not* the road to Inner Fitness. There are always more options available to us than we think. When we act out of fear or envy, or refuse to venture out and trust our own instincts, we live life as if we really don't have choices. We allow ourselves to be manipulated by outside forces, and shackled by the constraints of the "I Should" life. To free ourselves, we must recognize the critical role that we can play in deciding our range of options.

Shifting our perspective slightly, we can look at a rack of clothes and see not one but many flattering suits. Whichever we choose becomes the one we were seeking, simply because we chose it. Why? Because the specialness is in us, not in the clothes. I could have been happy and looked good in any number of the suits at Paul Stuart.

Achieving an awareness of choice is essential if we are to assert our individuality and seize control of our own lives. Although a liberating and powerful sense of individual freedom pervades every aspect of the Inner Fitness Program, this message is of such importance that it demands its own Tool for Living.

# INTRODUCING
# LIVING TOOL 3:
# THE CIRCLE AND DOT

The Circle and Dot (Fig. 3) is the symbol for what I call *the consciousness of choosing.*

In contemplating an action or a choice, we unconsciously draw a Circle around the Dots, or options, we believe to be open to us. The

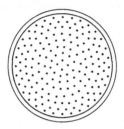

FIGURE 3. THE CIRCLE AND DOT

Circle defines the range of options; it is what we see to be the problem or question. The Dots are the potential solutions. This Tool for Living turns the process of free choice into a conscious activity, conditioning us to expand our horizons. The Circle and Dot is a reminder that:

> **For every action, choice, or decision we make, there is a circle full of alternatives.**

Every time we make a decision or resolve to take an action, we pluck a Dot out of our mental Circle. It is essential to realize that any Dot we choose—any action we take, any decision we make—is only one possibility out of a multitude of options. Conceivably, a Circle can contain as many Dots as grains of sand on the earth. No matter how often we say, "But I have no choice . . .", we still can take alternative paths of action if only we condition ourselves to dig deeper and ask the right questions. Even one additional fact or an ever so slight shift in perspective can open a wide array of new opportunities.

The Circle and Dot is also a visual reminder that *there can be more than one right choice.* There is no one perfect option just as there is no one perfect mate and no one fixed path for our lives. Among the choices surviving our preliminary screening, each has its advantages and disadvantages. It's dangerous to confuse searching for a good or quality choice with searching for a perfect choice. The former exists; the latter is a semantic fiction, a prescription for futility.

Seek perfection and you will find only stress, frustration, and inevitable disappointment. Your option-selecting process will become mired in doubt and confusion. Should you believe you've actually found the perfect mate or career or option, you soon will discover flaws and conclude you've made a terrible mistake. But instead of becoming flexible and ready to adapt to reality, you will continue to think that you must begin your quest for perfection all over again.

A quality choice is based upon intuition, solid experience, and sufficient information. It feels right. In the end, though, every choice is a calculated risk and no more than an educated guess.

Here's an example of how the Circle and Dot revolutionized my investment strategy and helped to increase my income. I had phased out of my own brokerage business and had put aside a cushion in guaranteed dollar savings. Now I was looking for ways to invest additional capital. I wanted more income than a bank offered and was willing to take what I call a "moderate risk" of about 20 percent. What was the appropriate investment? That was the Circle I created.

The first Dot to appear was blue-chip common stocks, owning them directly or through a mutual fund. Or I could turn my money over to a money manager to make the decisions. But I kept asking: What else was there?

At first, no new Dots appeared. But, by insisting and not taking "That's all" for an answer, more Dots showed up. I could pool my money with a group of friends to form a small syndicate and have more investment opportunities from a larger capital fund. I could back a conservative business venture. Again, I continued insisting on more options. I was forcing myself to be creative, as if creativity were as much a matter of determination as of innate ability.

Suddenly, I realized that I had been working under an assumption restricting my options: that all of my money had to be invested with the same degree of risk. But to achieve my goal, that wasn't necessary. I could invest 80 percent of my capital at low guaranteed returns and speculate with the remaining 20 percent (hoping to double or triple my investment). If I invested the entire amount at moderate risk, I figured I was risking 20 percent anyway. With my 80-20 approach, my overall risk was really no greater even if I lost my entire speculative 20 percent. In fact, my overall risk would be less since it would be partially offset by my guaranteed income, and my potential overall return was far greater.

Thanks to the Circle and Dot, I came up with an original plan to use highly speculative investments as a means of fulfilling my conservative goals. That plan resulted in a dramatic increase in my income. Using the Circle and Dot, you too can introduce adventure and daring into a controlled, conservative plan to get more out of life. Just keep searching for the missing Dot and keep asking, "What other way is there?"

Mary H., the young Boston mother in Chapter 2 who felt trapped by her circumstances, found her creative solution, her hidden Dot, when she realized that the problem she was facing was not solely her own but involved her family. When she brought her children into the decision-making process, she reached a new solution.

Les S., a struggling actor searching for ways to break apart from the competition, asks himself, "How can I improve my chances at an audition?" There appear to be no options. Stimulated by the Circle and Dot, however, Les develops an increased awareness of choice. He reaches down deep for an alternative. From now on, he decides to stay in character before, during, and after an audition. On his third try, his ingenuity so impresses the director that he lands a major part.

Whether we are trying to resolve business, personal, or political problems, it is essential that we avoid the pitfalls of decision making based on fact-starved options and ask the right questions.

## FORMING CIRCLES

In our search for answers, the precise way we phrase a question to ourselves will determine the number and nature of the Dots within our Circle. If you own only two blue dresses and ask yourself, "Which blue dress will I wear today?" then, obviously, only two Dots will swim within your pool of options. Asking, "What dress will I wear?" will increase the Dots, and asking more generally, "What should I wear?", will increase them even more. Ask, "What can I wear to make me look absolutely fabulous?", however, and, depending on how you feel about yourself and your wardrobe on that particular day, you may find a Circle with no Dots at all (a Circle usually accompanied by great anxiety).

> **Finding the right path of action means asking yourself the right questions.**

Asking the right probing questions can cut to the heart of a problem and help us break loose from the constraints of a confining Circle.

When the question is vague or premature, however, we become vulnerable to being unduly dependent upon others, accept simplistic solutions, make rash moves, or take no action at all. We must constantly be on the alert for changes in how we "read" or "size up" a situation. Consider the following case history:

Michele R. recently graduated from Boston College and was planning to settle in the Boston area. But when her boyfriend received a job offer from Bethlehem Steel in Pennsylvania, he expected her to accompany him. In response to the straightforward question, "Should I move to Pennsylvania with David?", her response was a quick, "Yes."

She was comfortable with David, their sexual relationship was intensely satisfying, she thought she loved him. She was unsure, however, whether moving away from her friends and her own job opportunities was the right thing to do at this time. So she dug deeper and asked herself some difficult, probing questions.

"Why do I want to accompany David? Am I too dependent on him, like I was on Jeff, my high school sweetheart? Am I afraid to be on my own? Is David afraid to be on his own? At twenty-one, am I willing to submerge my career and my ego to David? Do I really want to spend every day of the rest of my life with him?" And, finally, "What do I want to do?"

By asking these tough, basic questions, Michele realized that her decision was motivated more by fear than by desire. She was afraid of losing David not because she couldn't live without him but because, lacking self-confidence, she was afraid of living alone without someone to take care of her. In order to see how they really felt about each other, her final decision was to remain in Boston, visiting David as often as possible, and to reassess her needs and feelings and their relationship one year down the road.

Search out the most appropriate questions, permit your powers of perception an opportunity to function freely, be aware of your consciousness of choosing, and . . .

> **Become option-ready!**

Here are some specific ways to become option-ready: keep physically fit and active. (When our backs ache and our shoulders stoop under the weight of the world, we don't have the energy or desire to search out adventurous options). Let feelings of depression and disillusionment pass before seeking options. Keep Elmer's Glue in working order. One of the easiest and most effective ways of discovering new options is to delay your responses. When asked for a decision, say, "I want to sleep on it," or "I want to think it over for a while." Remember, there's no advantage to rushing into a decision, especially when you're the one who will have to live with that decision.

Visualize yourself as an artist carving your own life out of the raw material that is your environment. Recognize that every choice you make defines what you do *not* want as much as it does what you *do* want. This consciousness of choosing can be articulated in the following way: **"I am focusing on what I choose to see and I am creating my own perception of what is happening. I can change my view. I can look again and see or hear what I may not have seen or heard before."**

Not all of us want options, they can be pesky and annoying. Following the tried-and-true, narrow path often seems far easier emotionally. At one time or another, all of us have wished that, instead of having an unlimited choice of careers, we were locked into our father's trade, profession, or the family business. Why? Because options mean decision making, and that requires time, energy, personal commitment, and risk taking.

Seeking out options may indeed seem painful. It may even force us to leave behind something or someone or some old, comfortable belief. But, in the end, we'll find that such discomfort is a small price to pay for freedom, happiness, and personal growth.

Questions and choices are reflections of the person setting up the Circles and selecting the Dots. When it comes to being option-ready, nothing is more important than our commitment to the "I Choose" life. When we make that commitment, we connect to our feelings, our intuition, our "softer side," our faith in ourselves, and allow our own uniqueness to flow through us and influence our choices. This flow fires our consciousness of choosing and guides us to the right options. In so doing, we become a whole person, imbued with a sense of control and purpose. But if we lean toward the constraints of the "I Should" life, our range of options shrinks drastically.

## CHOOSING DOTS

Here are five cardinal rules to keep in mind when we are seeking options:

1. *Avoid searching for the perfect answer.* Believing in perfection is tantamount to believing that there is only one Dot within any Circle. (Remember my problem searching for the perfect suit at Paul Stuart?) For productive, practical problem solving, we must deal with process and probabilities rather than single-minded perfection.

Too often we consider choices as static, black-or-white alternative courses of action that exist out there in the world waiting to be uncovered. We can buy a house or not buy a house, we can have a child or not have a child. Actually, choices are parts of an ongoing, circular process made up of the questions we ask, the actions we take, and the evaluations of those actions, which then lead to new questions and more Circles and Dots. If at first our choices don't turn out quite the way we expect, we shouldn't give up hope. Each choice we make is a beginning rather than a dead end, because *the Circle and Dot is not a static concept but an ongoing, circular process, a picture of free will in action.*

2. *Welcome the ridiculous.* In exploring this option-creating process, we should never discard any option out of hand, no matter how bizarre or shocking it may seem. Often the most ridiculous possibilities help us to open our minds and guide our thinking into sound, creative solutions. Remember, the fantasy you have today could evolve into tomorrow's healthy reality.

3. *Don't pick the first option.* Options are like berries: the best are not always the easiest to pick or the first seen. When you go option picking, stay alert. Explore every area. Feel the adventure. Don't jump to the first conclusion.

4. *Keep insisting.* Stick with a problem and keep digging deeper. Your chances of breaking through to a new, creative solution will be increased dramatically. Keep asking yourself, "What am I missing? What other options do I have?" Remember, *there is always more.* Insist on an answer from yourself and don't take "There *are* no other options" for an answer.

5. *Look for differences.* In facing new situations, the old way of thinking influences us too much. It has us searching out similarities and leaping to place fresh, new experiences into musty, old cubbyholes,

compelling us to compare one thing to another. I believe that every experience is new and original. That excitement and opportunity derives from what is different rather than from what is similar. If you are an employer, in place of organizing employees strictly by their job classifications, you would be wise to see them with fresh eyes as unique, multifaceted individuals. Be alert for what makes a person different and you might uncover a wealth of hidden potentials wasting away in a static, de-humanized table of organization. When you walk along the same old street, instead of staring at the pavement, you should opt to see something new, to look up at the buildings you've passed by for years and notice, for the first time, the gargoyles on the warehouse facade, for example, or the date carved into the stone front.

## CREATIVITY AND THE CIRCLE AND DOT

Opening ourselves up to options and not taking anything for granted gives free reign to our curiosity, encouraging our creativity. As Bill Moyers has said: "You must never think that your most recent idea is your best or your last. You must be willing to keep searching your imagination and intuition for new versions and variations of that idea."

Only then will we develop creativity—the ability "to think in unhabitual ways," enabling us to "pierce the mundane to find the marvelous—or look beyond the marvelous to find the mundane." **At the heart of creativity is the ability to find new solutions by putting old bits of data together in new ways.**

As a Tool for Living, therefore, the Circle and Dot will help us change and expand the way we think about things. Though the Circle and Dot begins as a visual cue, with practice and conditioning it will become an attitude. We will find ourselves thinking: "There *is* another way."

## TOOLS FOR LIVING CONDITIONING EXERCISES: THE CIRCLE AND DOT

### Step 1: Forming Circles

1. ***Break out.*** In the business world, we call it "brainstorming." For us, breaking out means letting the Circles form freely. Think of a problem that's been bothering you. Maybe your stockbroker has been wrong more times than right, or your boss is on your case. Maybe you feel boxed in or confused. Relax, allow your mind free reign to ask whatever questions it will regarding the situation. Turn the problem on its head. Assume the other person's point of view.

Try to define the problem in a new way. Shatter the mold of your perceptions, attitude, and thinking.

2. *Track down the primary Circle.* Too often we waste our energy fighting the wrong battles. We scratch only the surface of our problems instead of dealing with the heart. Consider a problem occupying your mind. Ask yourself, "What is there about this problem that overrides all other primary considerations?" Dig deeply. Find the question or questions that tackle the problem head on.

## Step 2: Picking Dots

1. *Get visual.* Are you seeking a solution to a thorny problem? Draw a Circle on a piece of paper and fill it with Dots. Imagine a different solution for each Dot on the paper. Slowly your mind will relinquish its viselike grip on one idea. Options will appear where none were seen before. This visual exercise will help break the lock on your thinking and open up your creativity.

2. *Create more Dots.* Options don't just materialize out of thin air, they are the results of conditioning. If you are unhappy with any aspect of your life, make an effort to cultivate new options. Find new friends. Take up a new hobby. Change the way you dress or where you live. Develop a new skill. Every change in the way you approach life will open you up to new experiences and new solutions.

3. *Keep insisting.* You've been pondering an important question for days and believe you've exhausted all possible avenues of approach. At that moment, say aloud to yourself, "And in addition to that, what else is there?" Keep at it until you come up with something new and different. One minute you'll be swearing there is no other way, the next you'll be discovering a stream of new Dots.

4. *Welcome the ridiculous.* Think of a question or problem that is of current importance in your life. Consider the most outlandish, ridiculous answers and solutions you can imagine. Don't hold yourself back. Let yourself go. Break out! You'll be surprised at how it helps to liberate your thinking.

5. *Break the lock of perfection.* Is a deeply embedded belief in perfection paralyzing you and creating stress and frustration? Try this: practice on small, uncritical problems. Just when you see no viable choice, force yourself to plunge ahead and select one of the available options. Make a mistake, if necessary. Work to overcome your fear of making mistakes. In time, with practice, you will begin to break free of your fears and condition yourself to take risks.

6. *Rank your options.* Consider an important action you're contemplating taking. Before acting, make a list of all the alternative courses of action you can think of, then rank those options in order of preference. Does the option you rank as number one coincide with the action you plan to take? If not, reassess your decision.

## Step 3: Creating Six Important Circles

The skillful handling of the Circle and Dot reduces stress and stimulates vitality. Mastery comes with time and practice. Form the following six Circles and choose your Dots.

1. **Don't jump to conclusions.** A friend promises to phone on Friday night but doesn't. Annoyed, you form the Circle, "Why didn't my friend call?" Add the Dots. Don't restrict yourself to the reasonable, the rational. Allow your imagination to roam. After all, anything could have happened. By recognizing the reality of options, you may find that your anger has subsided and your perspective has changed.

2. **Break the routine.** Form a Circle of your daily activities, asking, "What shall I do today?" Add the Dots. Include those covering your usual routine then add new and different alternatives. Select an option that you would normally ignore, and act on it. The option could be baking a cake, surprising a friend, going to the zoo. Or it could be *not* doing something that you do every day. Don't take a shower, don't read the paper, don't answer the phone. Anything to break the routine. Acting on a new option will make you more aware of the power of your own free choice.

3. **Invent an option for a friend.** Sit down with one of your friends and explore a problem that he or she is currently facing. Help your friend formulate the Circle so that you get to the heart of the

problem. Now, both of you add Dots, stretch, and add more Dots. The Circle and Dot can work wonders within a relationship.

4. *Happiness is a Circle.* Form the Circle, "What would make me happier than I am today?" Add the Dots. Free yourself of your rationality. Let your verbal-free instincts take over. Get creative. Seek out fresh solutions to old problems.

5. *Success is a Circle.* Form the Circle, "What would make me more successful than I am today?" Add the Dots. After the easy ones —like winning the lottery—keep digging for more. Is there some personal habit that is holding you back? Are you working hard enough? Do you really want to succeed in what you are doing? Is there someone you respect who could help you? Keep digging. You know more than you think you know.

6. *Learn from the past.* Form a Circle around your past errors in judgment, those decisions you now look back on with regret. With the benefit of hindsight, consider what other alternatives you might have pursued and how they might have turned out.

# LIVING TOOL 4:
# THE NORTH STAR

Until now, we have emphasized the importance of delaying our responses, recognizing and acting on our inner warning signals, stretching our minds, locating new options, and have touched upon the need to take risks. Now we face the critical issue of direction.

A person with a sense of direction, someone who knows where he (or she) is going and loves what he is doing, is a rare and happy individual. We all know someone like that. Many of us look with envy upon those people who make a life's work out of what they love. They're superhuman or they're fantastically lucky, we say, sighing with resignation as we listen to successful people talk about how they're making millions doing what they would gladly do for nothing.

Where, though, do mere mortals like us turn to find the path toward self-fulfillment? How do we tap into the potential within us all? How do we locate and channel our energies toward those pursuits that will make us truly happy?

The answer lies in our next Living Tool, the North Star.

## INTRODUCING LIVING TOOL 4: THE NORTH STAR

POLARIS, or NORTH STAR: A bright, whitish-yellow star located less than 1° from the celestial north pole—the point in the sky directly above the earth's North Pole. Because it constantly marks due north for any observer in the Northern Hemisphere, this star has been used for navigation. The North Star can readily be located by following a line upward from the two stars of the Big Dipper or as the star at the end of the handle of the Little Dipper.

For as long as I can remember, I've loved to look up at the stars and ponder their mysterious beauty. I have always believed that the stars speak to us, that they shimmer with rays of hope and offer us a message and guidance.

The North Star in particular has always held a special fascination for me. What images and feelings that special star evokes! Beauty. Mystery. Magic. The Unknown. A beacon that ancient sailors, trusting to the heavens, relied on to chart their course across strange, black seas. When I look up at the North Star, I am reminded that there is more to life than just the grind of routine and the struggle to satisfy our material needs. I am reminded that there is something as grand and as majestic as that star within *us*. The North Star keeps my hope constant, as it does the passion with which I strive to achieve my dreams.

The North Star, therefore, is my fourth Tool for Living and the visual symbol of our dreams (Fig. 4).

The ability to dream is one half of nature's greatest gift to humankind. The other half of that gift, the most remarkable half, is our power to make those dreams come true. Thus the North Star reminds us not only that we must dream but that we must express and fulfill our deepest dreams and spiritual yearnings. If we do journey along a road guided by our dreams, our lives will be infinitely richer. We will have unforeseen opportunities. We will be inundated with positive emotional energy. Boredom, pretense, and frustration will be stripped from our lives. And we will enjoy a rebirth of self-respect.

FIGURE 4. THE NORTH STAR

There is within each of us a spiritual force, or will, urging us on to become the unique individual we were each destined to be if only we gave ourselves the chance. In my program, I encourage spirituality as an element natural to and essential for the growth of our individuality. This spirituality generates a faith in our ability to accomplish what we set out to accomplish, to fulfill our dreams, and, ultimately, to transcend ourselves and touch something beyond our own egocentric world. I call this experience of living, feeling, and doing "Applied Spirituality."

Applied Spirituality entails tapping into our spiritual core and making it an active force in our lives. It means plumbing the depths of our souls, bringing our true selves to the surface, and freeing our spirits. In so doing we become more vital and creative, and experience a new oneness with others and with the world around us.

The essence of the Inner Fitness Program is inner harmony. It is achieved when we apply our spirituality, working in harmony with properly channeled rationality, to the fulfilling of our life's potential.

How, in the face of all the demands upon our time and life, do we succeed in tapping our spiritual core and let ourselves be guided by our dreams? How do we turn the North Star from a charming symbol into a practical Living Tool with the power to direct and shape our lives?

The answer is simple. To follow the light of the North Star, all you need do is:

---

**Follow your fascination.**

---

Fascination transfixes us and holds us spellbound, arousing our most intense feelings and passions. Under its influence, we are drawn irresistibly to certain directions, led to specific activities, attracted to particular people. Find and follow those activities in life that fascinate you. Don't brush them aside as trivial or frivolous. Instead, let them lead you where they may and surround you in their magical aura. Your fascination is the pathway to your spiritual core. It puts you in touch with your deepest, truest self and, therefore, provides the key to following your North Star and fulfilling your dreams.

Fascination is more than mere interest or a passing fancy. It begins with curiosity and turns into something much more profound. It engages our total concentration. We become so absorbed that we lose all awareness of time and self. We forget to ask, "What's in it for me?" or "What should I be doing?" The deeper we move into and out of our selves, the more we create a fusion between our thinking and feeling and reach a state that brings out the best in us, makes us happiest, and is the most fertile ground for creativity. We feel the need to learn more, to explore, to create.

What fascinates each of us is utterly personal. My wife and I, for instance, are worlds apart. Zaida is fascinated by any piece of broken equipment. She can't wait to get her hands on it, take it apart, and try to fix it, which she does more often than not. When she is working with her hands, she becomes lost in concentration. The world around her disappears. She also follows the fascination of her hands through sewing, designing clothes, and gardening. By turning her fascination into a lifestyle, she makes each moment into a thing of beauty.

I, on the other hand, can barely open the hood of my car. Music has been an ongoing fascination in *my* life; a house without a piano seems empty and stifling to me. Despite my lack of formal musical training, I taught myself to play the piano and developed my own system for writing down the melodies I heard in my head. At sixteen, I began writing music and lyrics for songs. When I play and write music, I am lost in a world of joy and selflessness, expressing my very soul. Without music, my Sixth Sense Bells ring off the hook, warning me that I feel trapped and unfulfilled. A lifetime fascination, music has offered me an outlet for my inner spirituality and a means to express my individuality.

## TURNING THE NORTH STAR INTO A SKILL: MINI-FASCINATIONS

All of us are fascinated by certain ideas, objects, or activities. These may be as seemingly trivial as collecting seashells or as important as working to house the homeless. A fascination may last only a matter of minutes, or it may last a lifetime.

Even the most mundane of fascinations offers us a unique opportunity to tune in to our inner selves. The games, sports, or sometimes childish pursuits we enjoy can stimulate our most creative urges. Fantasies and daydreams can do the same. Like our nightly dreams, every fascination, even the most trivial, offers us a window to our most deepseated dreams and desires.

How do you turn the North Star into a living skill? By learning to . . .

**RESPECT AND DEVELOP YOUR MINI-FASCINATIONS.**

Acting on a fascination is not only a learning experience, it is one of the great joys of life. There is more than fun to be gained, however. By feeding our mini-fascinations with action, we condition ourselves to an action-oriented lifestyle. We get into good habits. We find out more and more about who we are, what we love to do, and what isn't right for us. Remember: you never know where a mini-fascination might take you.

Ever since he was a child, Scott Bruce had been fascinated by illustrated metal lunch boxes. Over the years, he collected thousands, from vintage Mickey Mouse and Davy Crockett boxes to Hopalong Cassidy, the first TV star to have his face grace a child's lunch box. Instead of abandoning his fascination, Bruce nourished it. He published a newsletter for other collectors, wrote a book on the history of the lunch box, and developed a price guide. He became the world's expert on the subject. He contacted museums and exhibited his collection. Single-handedly, he created a market that continues to grow. Some of his lunch boxes, which originally cost only a dollar or two, are now worth more than $600 each and his collection is valued at over $75,000. Money, however, was never the primary goal; it was only a bonus that resulted from following a fascination.

What was there about lunch boxes that reached down and touched Scott Bruce's spiritual core? Did those child's boxes express a longing for the simpler times of soda fountains and old-fashioned family values? Did they bring him closer to the American imagination? Whatever it was, it touched a universal chord and excited his passion. By nourishing his mini-fascination, Bruce developed a seemingly frivolous collection into a spiritually and financially rewarding life's work.

Angelin Girardi lived in the small farming village of Maquine located in the rolling hills and mountains of Osório, a southern province of Brazil. What made this slim mechanic, cabinet maker, and candy manufacturer so interesting was his unquenchable passion for life. Angelin had many mini-fascinations, one of which was his Model A Ford. Every free moment he could squeeze from his busy life, he spent tinkering with his car. He stripped it down and rebuilt it completely, repositioning the gas pedal between the clutch and brake. While devising a new braking system, he used a rock to hold down a metal spring. Lifting the rock released the spring, which in turn activated the braking system.

Every time he had to travel from Maquine to Pôrto Alegre, Angelin would drive his Model A. Although he had to stop every thirty minutes to let the engine cool and the trip took him many hours, he didn't care. Each trip offered him a chance to drive his car and visit with old friends along the way. When Angelin died, his body was carried to the cemetery in his Model A, in accordance with his final request! No one can measure the amount of joy he received from working on and operating that car. It was much more than an object to him; it was the physical manifestation of his own spirit, the object of the greatest passion in his hard life.

Consider the case of Alice R. As a child she loved to dance and almost attended a special school for the arts. As the years passed, though, she lost touch with that fascination and went on to a career as a psychiatric social worker at a mental health clinic. In time, she felt stifled by her job. The work, the atmosphere, the state bureaucracy wore her down until she felt as if she were dying. A profound sense of sadness pervaded her life. She grew more and more shy and introverted. She resolved to make a change. But what to do?

Searching for an outlet for her untapped energies, she began taking classes in anything that interested her. Finally, she tried a course in Anatomy and Kinesiology. Click! That was it! The combination of movement and health held a magical attraction for Alice. Her North Star, clouded over for years, began to shine brightly. She worked part time at the clinic and took a second job at a Fitness Center for five dollars an hour. Then she went to full time, began teaching prenatal and postnatal exercise classes, and became a certified fitness instructor. From there, she eventually became program director of a major weight control center, a job that she believes in and loves with passion.

Alice now bubbles with energy and enthusiasm. She feels confident. Her love life has improved. By following her fascination and unearthing her spiritual core, she made the real Alice emerge.

Following our mini-fascinations will help us to develop our North Star into a habit and a skill. This process doesn't always have to involve gut-wrenching career choices. It can lead us to follow pursuits out of pure joy that will round out and enhance our lives and help us achieve an all-important sense of balance.

## HOW PRACTICAL IS IT?

Words articulate our powers of reason. Fascination expresses our spiritual core. Combine the two into a harmonious partnership and we have a sound basis for charting a life course. Fascination points the way. Intelligent, critical thinking, combined with our innate creativity, helps us sort out our options and remove the obstacles in our path.

But is it practical to place so much importance on what appears to be so quixotic a notion as fascination? Yes. Absolutely.

As we all know, a person is most productive when working at something he or she loves. Following the fascination of our personal North Star will lead us into activities that we love. Therefore, to achieve the greatest degree of success, we must devote ourselves to those tasks that engage our passion and fascination. And that success may be measurable in dollars as well as in purely personal achievement.

The Bells warn us of what not to do. The North Star guides us into what is right for us to do. It is equally dangerous to our inner health to ignore either signal.

When we do not follow our North Star, our creative energies remain stifled. We become passive bystanders to our lives. We become bored and frustrated. Our healthy, positive energies may turn to passive pursuits, such as watching television or gambling, or to destructive outlets, such as drugs and alcohol. Many just daydream their lives away, wasting time and energy.

Throughout my years in investment sales, in training salespersons and running workshops, I have met literally thousands of people who ignore their fascinations and suffer the slow atrophying of their hopes, their goals, and their emotions.

Following your North Star is a practical and productive necessity. But how can we bring our dreams to life—make them come true—in a world that can be so brutal? The answer lies in learning how to blend our rational and spiritual sides and come to a dynamic compromise with ourselves.

# THE DYNAMIC COMPROMISE

Not all of us can follow our North Star completely and immediately to a new and lucrative career. Pressures of all sorts force us to temper our fascination with practicalities. We have to make a deal with ourselves. The secret is to make a dynamic compromise, not one that is thrust upon us or reached by default. It must be a timely, creative solution that reflects our own circumstances, needs, desires, and dreams, along with those of our family and friends. It is discovering that hidden Dot in a Circle of options. Instead of a new career, this compromise may entail devoting more time and energy to what I call "co-existent pursuits" (as opposed to the term "hobby," which connotes an activity we engage in "on the side" to help pass the time). It may mean biding our time in our current job until we secure the necessary training and funds to pursue our North Star on a full-time basis. Or it may mean sacrificing some time with our children in order to pursue a new career or new activity.

In any event, that dynamic compromise should be reached only *after* we have reached the practical limits of our fascination. Don't compromise first and dream later. We never get anywhere that way. The pressures to conform and stay put are much too great. Instead:

> **Follow your fascination for as far as it will take you and then, and only then, compromise.**

Take the North Star seriously. Give it your best shot. Find a way to make fascination a crucial, if not central, part of your life. Take a bold step. If this means leaving your home and quitting a lucrative job to pursue your dream of becoming an actress, then do it! When reality intrudes, take your bearings, and make a personal compromise between the rival pressures in your life. Just remember that your obligation to be true to yourself is at least as important as your obligation to others. Respect your "softer" side as a full and equal partner with your rational, practical side. Nowhere is this partnership more essential than in making a dynamic compromise with yourself.

No deal we make is set in stone, however. Never forget how much both the world and us change with time: priorities, fascinations, even our basic goals and dreams change. Your North Star of today will not be your North Star of tomorrow. In fact, in about 12,000 years, Vega rather than Polaris will become the prominent star nearest to the celestial pole, just as the star Alpha Draconis held that position some 4,300 years ago. Therefore . . .

---

Don't hesitate to renegotiate your deal.

---

That's what I did. When my fascination with investments, sales, and mutual funds had dimmed after years in business, I renegotiated the deal I had struck with myself, the compromise I had made between my fascination and my materialistic needs. One day, smack in the middle of a lucrative business venture, I paused, applied a Drop of Elmer's Glue, and did some quiet self-examination and reappraisal. I had a passionate desire to devote all my energies to the two things that had fascinated me since my childhood: music and writing. What was I waiting for? It was time to stop dreaming and start doing.

Success in business had provided me a degree of peace and security, but I didn't feel fulfilled. I was rich in material wealth but I felt poor in terms of spirit and fulfillment. I was in a rut, making money only for the sake of making money. This was not the pursuit that aroused my passion and love.

So I phased out of my lucrative business and decided to focus virtually all my energies on writing and music. This book is one of the fruits of that renegotiated compromise. The musical I am writing is another.

You, too, can find a way to turn your life into a personal triumph. Compromise when you must, but always strive to make your life so full and joyous that if you looked back you would say, "I wouldn't change a minute," instead of "If only I had . . ."

## LOVE, RELATIONSHIPS, AND FASCINATION

Follow your fascination and *you* become fascinating; your joy and vibrancy will become contagious. Your entire personality will be profoundly affected as you grow more in touch with your spiritual core. Being true to yourself, becoming one of the few with the courage to establish his or her own set of values and priorities, will fill you with an air of confidence, self-respect, and even power that others will find appealing. The more you enjoy the feeling of fulfillment and excitement that you gain from following your North Star, the less you will rely on superficialities and social poses. Your individuality will become more apparent to you and to those around you.

Following your own North Star will make you less self-absorbed and more interested in searching out the inherent adventure that lies in meeting new people. Not being self-centered will make you more attractive to others. Your relationships will become deeper and less demanding. You will discover what makes people unique rather than automatically stereotyping them. To be sincerely interested in what makes another person special is a wonderful way to make new friends or find a mate!

## THE LITTLE DROP OF MAGIC

At birth each of us is given a very special gift. A little drop of magic. It is that drop that makes me me and not you. That gives each of us our special thoughts, our special feelings and, most important of all, the special stuff out of which we create and actualize our own, individual dreams. These little drops were not unconditional gifts, though. Neglect them for too long and they evaporate into the air, leaving us no longer special and unique.

The moral of the story is clear: Follow the North Star, unleash the powers of that little drop of magic, and strive to be the special person you were meant to be.

# TOOLS FOR LIVING CONDITIONING EXERCISES: THE NORTH STAR

## Step 1: Finding Your Fascination

1. *List your current fascinations.* Make a list of things that already fascinate you, even the most trivial or mundane of mini-fascinations if those things truly engage you and arouse your passion. Don't neglect play, since our childlike activities can provide us access to some of our deepest and most creative urges. Think of those objects or activities that you can't imagine living without. Think of the activity to which your mind wanders when you're bored at work. Think of what gives you the most pride and self-respect. Think of what gives you the most fun in life.

2. *Recognize new fascinations.* Make a second list of activities you've never done but have always wanted to do. Include those subjects about which you know nothing but have always wanted to know more. Now take a close look at both lists and see if you can find a common thread running through them. Are there certain subjects, ideas, and/or activities that seem to get your heart beating a little faster? If you group them together, do they suggest a recurring dream? Remember, too, that fascinations are ends in themselves, not (like money or power) mere means to ends.

3. *Compare your life with your fascinations.* Now make a third list of the activities that actually occupy most of your time—your work, your children, et cetera. Compare this list with the previous two. Do they overlap? If not, most likely you are neglecting your fascinations and sublimating your true self in order to get by in the world.

4. *Having trouble?* If you're having trouble pinpointing your fascinations, focus in on what you like and what attracts your attention. What television programs do you watch? What magazine or newspaper articles catch your eye? What music do you listen to? Where do you go on vacation? Then ask yourself what it is about these objects or activities that inspires and arouses you. Isn't there a pattern?

5. *Play a game with yourself.* Try to remember the things that fascinated you as a child. Chances are, aspects of those things probably still fascinate you. Browse through a college catalogue to see what courses catch your eye. What sections of a bookstore do you spend the most time in? Focus mentally on your North Star, let your mind wander, and make a wish. By listening to your heart, you can identify activities you love and dreams you secretly harbor.

## Step 2: Following Your Fascination

1. *Nourish an old mini-fascination.* Take one ongoing mini-fascination one step further than you've ever taken it before. Allot extra

time for it. Read a book about it. Pursue it actively rather than passively. Notice how honest and unself-conscious this fascination makes you feel, how it engages your full concentration and seems to transport you to another, higher plane.

2. *Act on a new one.* Pick one fascination about which you know nothing. Make a concerted effort to learn more about it. Sign up for a course. Take a music lesson. Learn to mountain climb. Do something scary that takes courage and concentration, and gets your energies flowing.

3. *Act on a dream.* Focus in on one special dream that you've harbored for a long, long time, and imagine what it would really take to make that dream a reality. Take the first step, no matter how small, toward living out that dream. Even a tiny step in the right direction can help break you out of a rut. If you find that the reality doesn't match your dream, then adjust your dream or choose a new one.

## Step 3: Making the Dynamic Compromise

1. *Verbalize your deal.* Try to put into words the compromise that you are now making in your life. Are you devoting all your time and energy to tasks that bring you little or no joy? Are there things that you want desperately to do but, for practical, social, or material reasons, have been putting off? Make a list of the different priorities in your life. Come up with creative ways to blend your passion and

practicality into a lifestyle of dynamic compromise that you can live with.

2. *Be true to yourself.* Do you sincerely and honestly believe in the work you do? And does that work permit the real you to come out? If not, your Bells should be ringing because you are wasting your energies and fighting against your best, most productive self. What changes or adjustments in your current job would help you to be more satisfied and productive? Talk them over with your boss. Try to make your work even a little more harmonious with your real personality.

3. *Remember Angelin's car.* If it's just not possible to alter your work in any way, then seek out a co-existent pursuit to which you can direct your passion and energy. Don't flit from one interest to another, wasting your time in passive pursuits like watching television. Pick one thing that truly fascinates you and devote all your free time to it for the next week. See how much you can accomplish in that week. Notice how this fascination refreshes and energizes you.

4. *Take stock of your regrets.* Think of something in your life that you regret and wish you'd done differently. Ask yourself if indeed it really is too late. Isn't there something you can do now that will take the sting out of that regret and stop you from saying "If only . . ." for the rest of your life?

## Step 4: Renegotiating Your Deal

1. *Things change.*   Are you sure that your dreams haven't changed?
Is the fascination you followed in the past still a fascination today?
Or is there some other dream or passion which should now be
taking precedence in your life? Don't get stuck in a rut. Always be
ready and willing to renegotiate the deal you strike with yourself.

2. *Feel like a success.*   At this moment do you feel like a success in
your own eyes? If not, it's time to renegotiate. Think of what you
could be doing that would make you feel successful and fulfilled.
Now make a plan to help you actualize that dream.

## LIVING TOOL 5:
## THE CLOCK

*Time—he just keeps on movin',*
*Passing you by.*
*Time—he just never stops to*
*Lend you a hand.*
*He's a tough one, always takin' never givin'.*
*He's a rough one, always blamin' no forgivin'.*
*Such an independent soul.*
*No one's messin' with his role.*
*Time—movin' on, movin' on.*

*—From the song "Time" by V. Dishy*

As each minute ticks by, everything inside and around us is in a state of constant change. Yet, despite all the evidence, we continue to live as if we can stop the Clock.

There was a time when mankind *could* function without paying much heed to time and change. The serf in the Middle Ages had only to look to his past to know his future. Even the young freckle-faced American boy captured in the paintings of Norman Rockwell could safely assume that his life and goals would be like his father's, and that his children's goals would be like his. Nowadays, though, the interdependence of global economies, the rate of technological change, the increase in opportunities for personal growth and career potentials, the prevalence of divorce, the threat of cataclysmic nuclear war hanging over our heads, and the ease and speed of travel, make the future uncertain for everyone.

Once, violent climatic changes occurred in five-thousand-year intervals. Now, with acid rain, the depletion of the ozone layer, and other forms of environmental pollution, who knows how soon the next dramatic shift in weather patterns will occur?

Once, major technological advances occurred rarely and took decades to be absorbed into society. Now, we have to read the newspapers every day to keep up with the pace and complexity of technological change. What vast social changes will result from superconductors and advanced biological engineering in the near future?

In the past, personal and scientific thinking was premised upon the existence of immutable laws, fixed conditions, and predictable, recurrent patterns of behavior. Such a static view, however, can no longer cope with or explain today's social and scientific revolutions. The twenty-first century demands a new approach, one that applies process and change to our personal lives.

Unfortunately, too many of us today are ill-prepared and ill-equipped to cope with the social, political, cultural, and personal problems brought upon us by accelerating change. Our thought patterns and our decision making are still rooted in the past. Many of us have been left behind in the dust, hobbled by outmoded paradigms. Even our language betrays us. We often fall into the trap of believing that whatever we say, write, or read is plausible. We talk, for instance, of eternity and permanence as if they were real and achievable. That is why it is essential that we reclaim our thinking from the ephemeral constructs of our language and develop the skills and attitudes needed to enjoy and fully utilize time. Time, therefore, is the subject of our next Tool for Living.

## INTRODUCING
## LIVING TOOL 5:
## THE CLOCK

The Clock (Fig. 5) is a symbol of the process-oriented frame of mind essential for turning time into a living skill. And it is a visual reminder that, to achieve Inner Fitness, we must be fluid, flexible, and ready to adapt to change.

A friend of mine who is having minor coronary problems jokingly

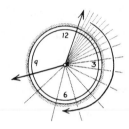

FIGURE 5. THE CLOCK

says that he doesn't buy green bananas anymore. For him, long range has become shorter and shorter. Although we need not be as acutely conscious of time as my friend, we all need to increase our awareness of the role of time and change in our lives. In order to find workable resolutions to our problems, we must take into account time's ongoing effects and the ongoing impact of our own actions. We must learn to adjust our thinking and decision making to take account of the Clock. To develop the Clock into a practical Tool for Living, I offer the following four techniques or guidelines.

## Guideline No. 1:

## Date the "Forever" Words

To keep our language under control and remind us that time means change, use an extremely simple device originated by Alfred Korzybski called "dating."

To those words, ideas, and statements that imply that the Clock does not exist, that suggest timeless generalities, add the date as a subscript. Write it, say it, hear it, visualize it, or think it, whichever most effectively helps you to tie words and concepts into time frames. Thus, when we say, "God," or "love," we should think "$God_{1990}$" and "$love_{1990}$" to distinguish them from "$God_{1890}$" and "$love_{1968}$."

Consider the labels "father" and "daughter": undated, these seemingly neutral, descriptive terms can lead to serious mistakes and misunderstandings. A father who persists in thinking of his daughter as a cute little tyke, as if she were still $daughter_{age\ 3}$ rather than $daughter_{age\ 18}$, fails to notice that she has become a woman. As a result, he risks alienating her and hindering her maturation process. Conversely, the grown daughter who never bothers to realize that her father is a man with doubts and fears and desires of his own or to see that her father has different needs and abilities at 50 than he did at 30, may never be able to establish a close, adult bond with him. Like all of us, both would do well to date their concepts and to see themselves (and others) as individuals who are continually changing, who cannot be stored away as if they were immutable commodities.

The simple act of dating and qualifying can make us feel better about ourselves and make us deal more successfully with our problems. Pronouncements such as "I'm not good at making friends" or "I hate my parents" cry out to be dated, if with nothing more than the words, "up until now." Undated, these statements promote acceptance and resignation: we are what we are, now and forever, so why waste time and energy trying to change? Dating, however, allows us to say to ourselves, "In the past, I've had a problem making new friends. Now I'd like to branch out and bring more people into my life." By the simple addition of a date, we open new perspectives and new options. We think: "I haven't gotten along well with my parents in the past, but I'm more stable and mature now, and they're much older, and I think it's time that I made an effort to reconcile our differences. After all, they raised me and loved me for many years. It's the least I can do for them."

"War" is a prime example of a word that cries out for dating. $War_{1812}$ and $war_{1914}$ used conventional weaponry and were won and lost. Should there be a next world war, $war_{2000}$, for example, it would be a nuclear holocaust with only losers. Date the word, and we realize how different the methods and stakes have become. Thus, dating the word helps us to think of war as something to evolve out of, rather than as something to plan for.

Consider the word "beauty." In America today, we're bombarded with the idea that youth and beauty are synonymous. In commercials and music videos, movies and television, magazines and fitness books, the young are portrayed as the aesthetic ideal. Instead of viewing beauty as a concept that changes with time, we see it as something that disintegrates over time.

If we dated "beauty," however, we would realize that it is not a single, static concept, reserved only for a particular age group, but that it takes many forms, ranging from beauty$_{child}$ and beauty$_{youth}$ to beauty$_{middle\ age}$ and beauty$_{old\ age}$.

Consider how two of the most beautiful women in the world have reacted to growing older and their different perspectives on time and change. In September 1984, both Sophia Loren and Brigitte Bardot turned fifty. For Ms. Loren, who was busy writing a book, creating a new perfume, and appearing in movies, her birthday was, "A wonderful thing. You are born, you grow older, and there's nothing wrong with it."

Ms. Bardot, however, entered her fiftieth year as a recluse, in a state of severe depression. "It's really tough to age," she said in a July 1984 interview. "It's half a century. Welcome to the senior citizen's club."

Clearly, she refused to accept the message of the Clock. She looked at the world in terms of timeless absolutes instead of seeing each new phase as an opportunity for growth and experience. On her last birthday, she attempted suicide.

Dating also applies to business. A well-meaning company president, firmly believing that he treats his workers "fairly," is shocked when his entire staff goes out on strike. Ten years ago, his work force consisted of twenty-five men, he drank beer with the boys on Friday night, and his employees responded positively when he treated them like his children. Now, his work force consists of three thousand people represented by a union, the company is under pressure from foreign competition, inflation has cut into workers' salaries, profits and productivity are down, and the president's paternalism is no longer sufficient or welcome. Paying inadequate attention to time and change, the president failed to recognize that "Fair Treatment$_{1990}$" and "Fair Treatment$_{1980}$" demanded two vastly different approaches.

We should even date ourselves because we are ongoing processes. There is no one, fixed personality that is Victor Dishy now and forever. There is only Victor$_{yesterday}$, Victor$_{today}$, and Victor$_{tomorrow}$. We may know where we have been and where we are, but we cannot know where we will be going. That's why the Clock opens us up to unlimited opportunities for growth.

## Guideline No. 2:

## Think Time Spans

Many of us pay lip service to the effects of time but still cling to a belief in foreverness. We say, "Nothing is forever," but still believe that "love is everlasting." Such conflicting views are difficult to avoid because of the near impossibility of thinking and talking about things in flux. We can't count on tomorrow being an exact replica of today, yet we also can't live from day to day with the feeling of imminent change. In order to function effectively in this world, we need to find a practical compromise between the need for stability and the acceptance of change. Thinking in Time Spans enables us to do this by cutting the impact of time into manageable, bite-sized bits. We anticipate stability, but only for limited periods of time. Setting a Time Span is setting our Clock to ring an alarm at a fixed date in the future. At that time we look about to see how personal, social, cultural, and technological changes have affected our lives, our goals and our plans.

Often, when a college student is asked about her career plans and how she expects to earn a living, she becomes nervous and confused. Why? Because she assumes that she has only one choice and one shot at a career. She believes that her decision must be absolutely right or she will be doomed for life. That student should be conditioned in the lesson of the Circle and Dot (that there is no one "perfect choice") and to think in terms of Time Spans (of, say, three to five years). Suddenly the pressure is dramatically decreased. Now the young student can picture that first career as only one step on a lifetime track that could lead to two, three, or even more careers. Her decision about that first job no longer becomes a do-or-die, make-or-break proposition. With the pressure off, she may even choose to do something she likes rather than something she thinks she "should" do.

In considering our futures, we should think in terms of Time Spans of, say, five years rather than trying to plan for a lifetime. Our careers and relationships should be updated and reevaluated at regular intervals so that we can keep pace with the facts of change.

In setting out a company's marketing strategy, a business executive would do well to spell that plan out on paper, date it, and then give it a Time Span. Clinging to outdated and undated strategies has been the downfall of many a company.

## Guideline No. 3:

## Consider the Ripple Effect

Imagine the following: you're driving your Honda at seventy miles per hour down a straight road. Directly ahead of you, only a couple hundred yards away, is a brick wall. You say to yourself, "No problem. Everything is fine. I haven't hit the wall yet." So, you drive on at full speed until you crash headlong into the brick.

Sounds silly, doesn't it? Who could be that stupid and naïve? Yet many of us lead our lives at full speed without giving a thought to the brick wall just ahead, rationalizing our extraordinary self-delusion by saying, "I'm too busy with the present to think about the future; it will just have to take care of itself." Such an attitude smacks of the "I Should" life and blatantly disregards the vital role process plays in our lives.

As a society and as individuals, we tend to act as if past, present, and future are all independent of each other. Our government spends more and more money on defense, ignoring the warnings about trade imbalance and deficits, only to wake up one morning to find that the budget deficit has crippled our economy. As the saying goes, all that we learn from history is that we learn nothing from history.

Let's stop and consider Past, Present, and Future, or what I call the PPF relationship, in human terms. The "Past" is a misleading label. For human beings, the past isn't something that's simply over and done with; we carry it with us every day of our lives. It is a vital, functioning part of our present and a major determining factor in our future. The "Present" is not an isolated moment; it includes both our accumulated history and the seeds of our tomorrow. As for the "Future," it exists in isolation only on the calendar. It is with us right now. Outside events clearly affect our lives but, whether we realize it or not, we make our own future out of our past and present. We would do well to deemphasize the labels Past, Present, Future, and think of life as a single ongoing process. Do that, and the Clock becomes much more than just a mechanism for telling the time of day.

Using the Clock and thinking in terms of the PPF relationship, we will develop the habit of considering the *Ripple Effect* of our actions and decisions. We know, or think we know, what the immediate effects of our choices and actions will be. But more often than not we fail to project the long-term consequences of those actions and fail to consider the full range of events or conditions we may be triggering. For example, whereas once unions were the bastions of fair policy and workers' rights, some unions have become single-minded forces for higher wages and benefits. By considering only "What's in it for me today?" instead of looking to the long-term welfare of the company, some unions have left their employers vulnerable to acquisition, foreign competition, or bankruptcy. Such self-defeating tunnel vision ignores the Ripple Effect.

Sometimes we have to listen to our Bells and act just on our instincts. Sometimes we have to follow our North Star, seize the moment, and enjoy it for what it is. I'm not suggesting that we sacrifice the present for the future. What I *am* suggesting is that a sensible, productive orientation toward time requires a balance between making the most of the here-and-now and looking ahead, between immediate gratification and long-term goals. Some of the greatest pleasures in life, such as developing an art or skill; building a sleek, muscular body; or establishing a firm financial base, require short-term sacrifice for long-term gain. Other pleasures, such as enjoying a sunset or tasting a favorite food, require only the ability to savor and experience a sensual delight. To fully utilize the Clock as a Living Tool, we must learn to walk that tightrope between the present and the future just as we seek a constant balance between our thoughts and our feelings.

## Guideline No. 4:

## Temper Those Expectations

Just as $E = MC^2$ is a key formula for modern physics, so $R = E + S$ is the key equation for our personal defense against a barrage of emotional dangers. In our equation, R stands for Reality, Ec for Expectation, and S for the inevitable Surprise. Because we live in a world in the process of change, we can't always get today exactly what we got yesterday; the world doesn't always turn out just the way we expect.

Because the baby boomers of today grew up in a prosperous era of unparalleled economic growth, they don't really understand this equation. They expected to go to college, work hard, and have as much if not more material wealth than their parents. Unfortunately, as a result of inflation, foreign competition, and the budget deficit, the reality of their attainments has turned out to be surprisingly and discouragingly different. Although this generation may earn more on paper than their parents, their buying power is less. Houses and cars are vastly more expensive, and a young couple needs two full-time incomes to finance a reasonable standard of living. The baby boomers are facing the inevitable surprise that comes with change.

If we think that reality will conform exactly to our expectations, we are in for a real surprise.

# TIME - ACTION - CHANGE

For Inner Fitness, it is essential to realize that the qualitative aspect of time is far more important than the quantitative. Time should be measured by what we *do,* not by the rotation of the earth. Time is the dimension from which we create our destiny. What counts is what we make of time. Like clay in a sculptor's hands, time is the creative material with which we shape our lives.

When we think of "yesterday," we don't visualize the hands of a clock, we think of what we did, of changes that occurred, and of what was new and different. Time, change, and action, therefore, are not separate and distinct concepts but run together in a continuum. Contrary to popular belief, we *can* make up for lost time. How? By packing sixty-one seconds of real living into a minute, or two calendar years into twelve fruitful, challenging, active months.

Have you ever noticed that athletes and dancers never appear to be rushing, no matter how fast they move? They always appear under control when they perform. This energy-efficient rhythm and sense of timing is what the Clock and the entire Inner Fitness Program aim to provide. Proper use of the interrelated Tools for Living can condition us to healthy life rhythms that will help us break entrenched, self-defeating habit patterns. Elmer's Glue is especially valuable in conjunction with the Clock because it encourages our spending more time on the stress-releasing wordless level.

For a total sense of Inner Fitness, we cannot try to stop the clock and fight change. We must accept ourselves and our environment as ever-changing. Do this and we become more in sync with ourselves and, thus, with others.

## RELATIONSHIPS OVER TIME

Dating our words and thinking in terms of Time Spans is vitally important to relationships. When two people with the right chemistry meet and share common interests and goals, they form a bond and expect that bond to be long-lasting, if not lifelong. As time passes, however, each partner changes, for better or worse. So does the way they relate to each other. Only by paying sufficient attention to the Clock can two people sustain and grow in a relationship. Let me illustrate by citing two examples of partner relationships over time.

1. *Sexual Partners.* All couples, regardless of the partners' ages, experience changes in their sex lives. The passion that characterized their

courtship and first flush of love quite naturally fades in the face of pressures from work, demands from children, and the familiarity of constant companionship. Changes in a person's finances, job satisfaction, appearance, and self-esteem, as well as in age, all impact on his or her sex drive.

Couples who fail to think of sex in terms of the Clock threaten their relationship by seeking self-destructive explanations for the natural ebbs and flows of the sex drive. They blame themselves, each other, or their relationship. They question whether they love each other. They permit sex to become an issue that creates a gulf between them rather than an act that brings them closer together.

Over the span of time, a healthy sexual relationship requires each partner to date the sex drive and accept the naturalness of change. $Sex_{20}$, $Sex_{35}$, $Sex_{50}$, and $Sex_{65}$ are different but by no means less pleasurable experiences, just as $Sex_{married\ 1\ year}$, $Sex_{married\ 5\ years}$, and $Sex_{married\ 25\ years}$, will be different but no less physically and emotionally satisfying. A sexual relationship is not static but must be viewed as an evolutionary process to which both partners must adapt. By paying heed to the Clock, we can sensitize ourselves to the changes inherent in an ongoing sexual relationship. With imagination we can learn to transform our erotic familiarity with each other into positive feelings of sexual understanding, acceptance, and security and so continue to deepen the passion of our love.

2. *Business Partners.* Business partners who ignore the Clock are courting emotional and/or economic disaster. For two people to succeed together in business, they must date and attach Time Spans to all the key elements of their joint venture. They must dig below the surface to explore potential problems and disagreements that could arise over time—everything from how they will handle the growth of the business to the role each of their spouses will play in the partnership. They should spell out in the partnership agreement current issues, such as the division of labor and responsibility and the way profits and expenses will be divvied up. And they should establish *in advance* how they will handle the eventual dissolution of the business.

For a joint venture to succeed, both partners must agree to a regular reassessment and reevaluation of the partnership in order to be sure that their goals and styles and personalities continue to mesh. In a business relationship, as in any partnership, it is also important to remember the Ripple Effect, and to temper our expectations. Following these guidelines will lead us naturally into constructive patterns of questioning and will help us resolve problems before they escalate into serious and perhaps insoluble conflicts.

# TOOLS FOR LIVING CONDITIONING EXERCISES: THE CLOCK

## Step 1: Dating Your Words and Thoughts

1. ***Date the "forever" words.*** Develop the habit of dating your own thoughts and words, especially those that imply timelessness. Question the validity of your own undated and unqualified assumptions. Do it in your business as well as in your personal life.

2. ***Listen for undated words.*** The next time you are in a conversation, listen for words or statements that suggest an unqualified and unchanging reality. These are the statements that often incite conflict and disagreement. Sidestep such conflicts by keying in on and pointing out the temporal nature of such remarks.

3. ***Date your self-criticism.*** List those personality traits you don't like in yourself, then date each of them to make you aware that these traits are not permanent. How did these same traits manifest themselves five years ago? Make a note to reevaluate them six months from now. If you try hard enough, you can change even your most ingrained habits.

4. ***Date a friend.*** Think of a friend you have known for a number of years and ask yourself how that person has changed

over the past years. Consider his or her appearance, relationships, interests, goals. Add date subscripts to the different manifestations of that person's changing personality. Become aware that, in order to sustain a long-term friendship, you must be sensitive to and willing to adjust to the changes your friend will undergo. Do this specifically with your personal and business partners.

5. *Date yourself.* Determine how much you have changed in the past and consider how much you can change and grow in the future.

6. *Date your dreams.* As we saw in the North Star, even our dreams must be reassessed and reevaluated over time. Review some of your recent and most long-standing fascinations. Date them. Are they still applicable today? Do you think they will continue to be fascinations for you tomorrow?

## Step 2: Thinking Time Spans

1. *Set Time Spans.* Instead of always worrying about your "future," review your life at five-year intervals. Where were you five years ago compared to where you are now? Where do you want to be in the next five years? What job do you want to have, where do you want to live, whom do you want to be with? Set a Time Span and make a concrete plan. Setting Time Spans will take the pressure off you and, hopefully, free you to focus your energies on a practical plan for achieving your objectives.

2. *Lay out goals.* Write down your personal and career goals and give them a Time Span. Resolve to reevaluate your situation at the

end of these spans, taking into account changes that have occurred in you and in the world around you.

## Step 3: Considering the Ripple Effect

1. *Consider the PPF Relationship.*   Are you one of those people who tries to forget the past and not think about the future? Our pasts and futures are always with us, however, no matter how much we try to deny them. "Living for the moment" is as much a long-term goal as "planning for retirement." Use the Clock to help remind you that your present life is only part of an ongoing continuum. But beware! The actions you take today will affect and determine your future.

2. *Project into the future.*   Think about an important decision you are about to make or an important action you are about to take. Consider fully the implications of different courses of action: How will those courses impact on you, your family, your friends, and your career over the next six months, the next year, the next five years? Remember that everyone around you will also change during those Time Spans. Understanding the Ripple Effect will help you make wiser and more thoughtful decisions.

## Step 4: Tempering Your Expectations

1. *Expect the unexpected.* As Murphy's Law puts it, what can go wrong—will! So make a contingency plan, just in case something comes up or anything goes wrong with something you plan to do in the future. Set aside a reserve of energy, time, and dollars, if necessary, to deal with the unexpected. Do this regularly and you won't be as disappointed when things don't turn out quite the way you planned.

2. *Use your imagination.* With the right attitude and a little imagination, a failed plan can be turned into a golden opportunity. Think of some unexpected event that recently stymied one of your undertakings. Now devise ways you could have turned that surprise glitch into an adventure or an opportunity.

# LIVING TOOL 6:
# THE BOW TIE

*Things aren't all so tangible and
sayable as people would usually have
us believe; most experiences are unsayable,
they happen in a space that no word has
ever entered.*

—*Rainer Maria Rilke*

Invariably, as I move along in the ongoing process of decision making, I must relate to another person. It often comes as a shock, though, to realize that while I have been busy sorting out facts and feelings to arrive at perceptions, opinions and decisions, that other person has been doing the very same thing. It can be an even greater shock to discover how very different our perceptions and opinions are

from others, even though both began with the very same set of so-
called facts. No wonder communication is so very difficult. As stated in
Chapter 3, words themselves are the major obstacles to effective communication. We insist upon endowing them with objective universal
meaning, as if the communication process is nothing more than the
delivery of a noncontroversial telegram that carries the exact same
meaning and impact for both sender and receiver. This simplistic view
of communication, however, falls far short of reality.

Clearly, the same words spoken by different people in different
contexts to different audiences can convey totally different meanings.
A general who yells "Fire!" to his troops means something completely
different from the man who yells "Fire!" when he smells smoke in his
apartment; and he, in turn, means something very different from the
delinquent who yells "Fire!" in a crowded movie theater when he
knows perfectly well that there is no fire.

Undigested words are like raw food. Just as raw food has value only
when it is digested, so words attain significance and meaning only
when they have been "digested" by the mental processes of a human
being. **The process by which you fuse and integrate written sym-
bols and actions with your purposes and feelings results in an
end product that creates what we call** *meaning*. **What a word
means to** *me*, **therefore, may bear little resemblance to what it
means to you.**

To move beyond language communication, where *words* talk to each other, to organic communication, where *people* talk to each other, we must surrender the myth that words alone can express what we feel and think to another person. Instead, we must accept that:

> **Communication is not the static transferring of data from one person to another but the sharing of personal perceptions.**

Our lives would be much more livable if people said, "Let us share our perceptions," instead of "Let me tell you what I think" or, even worse, "Let me tell you how it is."

Becoming aware of this new model for communication is a major step toward Inner Fitness. Equally important is turning this awareness into a practical skill. It isn't enough to tell someone to "share perceptions" or "be a good listener." That makes about as much sense as telling someone who has never touched a keyboard to "be a good pianist." How do we gain a deeper understanding and a mastery of this process of meanings making? We must look below the surface at what happens when we talk with another human being and transform the communication process into a working relationship.

The starting point is finding a new "unit of communication" to replace words. This unit is represented visually by the Inner Triangle (Fig. 6).

Just as an iceberg shows only one-eighth of its total mass above

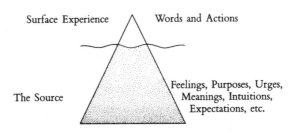

FIGURE 6. THE INNER TRIANGLE

water, only the words and the actions in my diagram—the tip of the iceberg—are visible above the watery surface (indicated by the wavy line). What remains hidden from view are the far more important—potentially dangerous or beneficial—forces that lie beneath our words: our personal purposes, feelings, and meanings.

The Inner Triangle symbolizes the fusion of words, actions, and all that lies beneath our words, to form the new unit of communication. *When we speak, we transmit this integrated totality; when we listen, we receive, consciously or subliminally, the information contained in the speaker's Inner Triangle.*

Nathaniel Branden, the noted psychologist, alludes to this organic fusion in *The Disowned Self:*

Included in a person's "experience" of some event is the way that event or aspect of reality is perceived by the person; the way it is judged, evaluated or interpreted, and how it is responded to emotionally and physically. . . . We can, by a process of abstraction, differentiate perception, evaluation and response, but it seems that the brain records these elements as an integrated unity, as part of one experience.

The Inner Triangle reminds us not to separate words from who is saying them, when and where they are spoken, and why they are being said. For true communication and understanding of the whole person, we must allow our underlying meanings, purposes, and feelings to come through; we must also search for them in the other person. When I listen only to your words and assume that I know what you mean, I risk misunderstanding and interpersonal friction. It is difficult to accept that words do not necessarily mean the same to us as they mean to others. Nor is it easy to resist believing that words can be innocently objective. Resisting these tendencies is the primary task of our new and final Tool for Living.

# INTRODUCING
# LIVING TOOL 6:
# THE BOW TIE

The Bow Tie (Fig. 7) is a visualization of the meeting of two Inner Triangles. It represents the interaction of one person with another, with the knot of the Bow Tie being the surface interchange—the supposedly common ground of words and actions. At the points where the two triangles touch, each person contributes to and takes from the conversation his or her personal blend of words, meanings, purposes, and feelings. Focusing on the picture of the two Inner Triangles meeting point to point reminds us to look beneath the surface of words and to notice what is going on within the other person and within ourselves. In doing so, we become more skillful listeners, perceivers, and communicators.

Whenever two people interact, a Bow Tie is formed. For instance, consider the complexity of greeting someone with the seemingly uncharged words, "How are you?" What you mean by this expression, the purpose behind your saying it, the tone of your voice, and the feelings that lead you to say it, taken altogether as a unified whole,

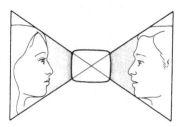

FIGURE 7. THE BOW TIE

form your Inner Triangle. The other person's response—a few words, a nonverbal nod, a casual wave of the hand—similarly reveals only the tip of his or her Inner Triangle.

But *how* can we discover what is really going on inside another person's Inner Triangle? At times, we all go out of our way to conceal the true feelings beneath our words, perhaps because we're shy or don't want to hurt someone's feelings or we're cunning or in a politically sensitive position. The fact is, we can *never* know exactly what's going on inside another person. We can, however, become aware that *something* is going on and make our best effort to get in closer touch with the meanings and purposes inside that other person's Inner Triangle.

In order to do that, I offer the following suggestions:

1. If you want to know what a person is feeling or thinking or what purpose he or she has in mind—*ask*. You'll be surprised at how a direct question can disarm even the most reserved of people.

2. If you meet resistance, try being open and honest yourself. Expose your own beneath-the-surface activities—your meanings and feelings —even if they're not complimentary. Your own honesty may just trigger honesty in your interlocutor. Being forthright is a key to open communication.

3. Try what I call, "going parallel." Venture and then verbalize a guess as to what the other person is thinking or feeling. The guess might make the other person disagree sharply and thus reveal his or her true feelings. Or it may elicit a hearty agreement.

4. Pay attention to the other person's body language. Does he look you in the eye when he speaks or is he looking to the ground or off to the side? Are her hands relaxed and open or is she clutching them defensively to her body or playing with them nervously? Look for visual clues that will give you insight into the other person's state of mind.

Let's now consider some more charged and less perfunctory exchanges that involve the Bow Tie.

## "Would you make me a drink?"

Jennifer V. is dead tired. After having worked a full day, prepared dinner, and put the kids to bed, she's finally sunk down into the couch for a well-deserved rest. "Would you make me a drink?" she asks her husband, Kevin.

Nose in the paper, he replies, "In a minute," in a distracted tone and goes on reading.

Jennifer explodes with anger. "Forget it! I wouldn't want to disturb you," she says sarcastically. "I'll make it myself."

Kevin looks bewildered. "What's eating you?" he asks. "I *said* I would get it."

What did Kevin do wrong? He made the classic mistake of interpreting and responding to his wife's words literally instead of tuning in to the hidden message behind the words. Jennifer may have wanted a drink but, more importantly, she wanted a little attention, a little babying, a little loving care. By being insensitive to the real-life relevance of Bow Tie understanding, Kevin walked blindly into an argument. Ignore the Bow Tie too often and the little cracks in a relationship can develop into major splits.

### "I need you and want you."

Bob C., a young attorney, in proposing marriage to Joan M., a management consultant, tells her that he needs her and wants her. The words certainly seem clear, quite positive, and even romantic. Joan thinks she is hearing Bob's expression of his need for a soul mate and her own romantic version of idyllic true love. And, as we all know, love conquers all. So they married and everything was sweetness and light . . . for a while. A very little while.

Unfortunately, though, it took Joan seven long spirit-sapping years to discover that Bob's "I need you" meant that he needed her as a housewife, a sex partner, a social ornament, and as caretaker for his children by a previous marriage! The marriage ended in a bitter and traumatic divorce.

What went wrong? How did it happen that two intelligent people fell victim to such a serious difference of interpretation? The fault lies in our tendency to bumble through life without adequate understanding of the different meanings that words convey and without sufficient recognition that we do not communicate with words alone.

Had Joan known about Bow Ties and looked at her own Inner Triangle, this is what she would have found:

HIS WORDS: I need you and want you.

HER MEANING: He needs and wants *me* rather than anyone else. Therefore, I am important to him. I am someone special. No one else wants me. I am lonely and he can't live without me. We will grow closer as we grow older.

HER PURPOSE: To find a soul mate and a companion to share and complete her life.

HER FEELINGS: Romance, the craving for security, fear.

Had Joan delved into Bob's Inner Triangle, this is what she would have found:

HIS WORDS: I need you and want you.

HIS MEANING: I need a woman to fill out my life and satisfy my needs. I want someone to care for my children. I need a wife in order to get ahead in my job. I'm tired of playing the field and want to settle down again.

HIS PURPOSE: To acquire a wife as a possession, a valuable asset to be paid for with the promise of financial security.

HIS FEELINGS: Sexual attraction, greed, the search for security.

Had she been aware of the Bow Tie process, Joan would have been able to uncover her own meanings and purposes. Certainly she would have questioned Bob more closely as to his. In a healthy communication effort, the "I need you" conversation would have progressed to an exploration of just what Bob meant by his words. It would have been the beginning rather than the end of communication between them.

### "Let's dance."

Sandra K., an editor of a leading fashion magazine, is attending an industrywide dinner with her husband, Freddie. "Let's dance," she whispers to him, grabbing hold of his hand. "I don't feel like it," he responds. "I don't like the music."

Soon they are bickering and snapping at each other, embroiled in one of their usual arguments. Finally, Sandra storms out of the ballroom followed by her quiet, rational, and self-righteous husband.

How could an awareness of the Bow Tie have helped this couple? Had Freddie tried to hear the personal meaning his wife gave to those words, he might have realized that his wife's desire to dance expressed her wish to be visible at the affair and her desire to make industry contacts. Had he been sensitive to her needs and aware of how important the event was to her, Freddie could have made the small sacrifice of dancing, despite his distaste for the activity.

On the other hand, Sandra could have been more sensitive to her husband. Knowing he didn't like to dance, especially in public, and that he was already uncomfortable in his role as "spouse" at her business gathering, she might have made an effort to put him at ease. She might have said, "I know you don't want to dance, but it's important to me to appear very social at this gathering. If you'll dance with me now, I promise that I'll go with you to the softball game on Saturday." By being open about her motives and willing to compromise, Sandra could have encouraged communication and helped to avoid a confrontation.

# THE  BOW  TIE  AND  SALES

Communication is at the heart of persuasion. We often are in the position of having to "sell" our ideas or products or our beliefs to another person. To close any sale, it is essential that the seller choose the most appropriate approach to motivate his clients to buy. He must also listen closely to the feelings and fears beneath his clients' words.

Logic is not always the most effective approach. In fact, the logical and rational approach often proves to be the wrong one. Some time ago, trying to interest a prospective investor in a new joint venture, I was about to offer the deal on a 60-40 basis—with the investor receiving the larger share. The client, though, seemed extremely wary and skeptical. Everything he said indicated that he was afraid of being taken advantage of, and that his focus was on feelings, not rationality. My Bells rang. I paused and tuned in to his Inner Triangle.

I observed his body language and noticed obvious signs of his fear and discomfort. I shared my thoughts about his fears with him. That led him to talking about a bad experience he had in the past with a joint venture. I asked him several pointed questions and his answers convinced me that it was essential that whatever proposition I offered had to provide him emotional reassurance. Glimpsing his Inner Triangle, I made a last-minute decision that my offer would sound more persuasive if I offered him a 50-50 split, 10 percent less than I'd planned! Fifty-fifty had a reassuring ring of fairness to it: what you make, I make. What you lose, I lose. We're in this together. Had I offered him a 60-40 split, on the other hand, he might have asked himself, "Why not 70-30?"

As it turned out, he went along with the venture.

Using the Bow Tie and tuning in to the other person's Inner Triangle not only helps us become better communicators, but also better persuaders. And that can make us more powerful and successful.

By now it's clear, I hope, that when two individuals with different backgrounds and wide variations in immediate needs and purposes meet, the words they speak rarely "mean" the same to both. Remember, each carries the baggage of his or her specific past, crammed with personal prejudices, biases, tastes, values, religious and political opinions, and preconceived ideas. Each has his or her own set of skills, level of intelligence, cultural background, and particular neurotic patterns. Considering all this, can we ever be certain that we understand what someone is really saying, or know for sure how what *we* are saying is being understood?

## SHIFT FOCUS

The Bow Tie and the Semantic Bells work hand in hand. To communicate with another person, it's essential to ascertain on what level each party is dealing. Am I talking in specifics while you're thinking in concepts? Or am I talking in conceptual terms while you're overrun by your feelings? If so, the chances of us communicating with each other are as slim as if I were on the first floor yelling up to you on the ninety-second floor. For a true sharing of perceptions to take place, it's essential to be ready, willing, and open to shift our focus not only from specifics to concepts to wordless sensitivity, but back and forth from an inner to an outer orientation.

Too often we only pretend to pay attention to what the other person is saying and feeling: we just continue to focus on how *we* feel, what something means to *us,* and what *our* purposes may be. To learn what's really happening within that other person, we must sacrifice our egocentricity. Only by being flexible and open will we be able to put ourselves in sync and make genuine contact with each other. And that's what life's all about—communicating our true thoughts and feelings to each other so that we can share the joys and pains of life, achieve our goals, and overcome our loneliness.

A simple shift in perspective can change our total outlook on a situation and our entire perception of what is being communicated. Remember . . .

> **Words don't talk, people talk.**

Applying the Bow Tie as a Living Tool until it becomes second nature conditions us to go beneath words and make those simple shifts in perspective that open us to the power and control that we have over our own lives—to the "I Choose" lifestyle.

## THE BOW TIE AND INTUITION

The role of intuition in interpersonal communications cannot be underestimated. To develop our Bow Tie awareness and enhance our communication skills, we must not only think and probe on a conscious level, but we must rely on our instincts and our "softer side." When we try to tune in to another person's Inner Triangle, we should use the intuitive tools—Elmer's Glue and the Bells. They will help us "get a read on" the thoughts, meanings, purposes, and feelings behind the mask of words. Because genuine communication takes place beneath and beyond words, we must pay attention to our inner signals and listen to our hearts. Only then will we develop the chemistry necessary to become "sympatico" with those to whom we wish to communicate, and achieve a closeness with them.

## THE BOW TIE AND INNER HARMONY

Often we find ourselves feeling one way and acting another. To attain Inner Fitness, we must work constantly at closing this gap: we must be honest with ourselves. When we do use words, let's have them express our true feelings. Let's talk more about our purposes and our underlying goals and intentions. Doing so will lead to a greater appreciation of language skillfully and artfully used. Let's allow the verbal pause encouraged by the Drop of Elmer's Glue to open the way for our feelings to emerge, honestly and freely, through the tone of our voices, our facial expressions, our body gestures. Let's allow the Bow Tie to lead us not only to better communication but to a deep sense of inner harmony.

What if you find yourself in a relationship or a job situation that demands, in the name of practicality, that you squelch your true feelings? Start thinking of ways to change your perception or change the situation. If this is impossible, there is only one choice left: move on!

# TOOLS FOR LIVING CONDITIONING EXERCISES: THE BOW TIE

## Step 1: Tuning in to the Inner Triangle

1. *Get visual.* The next time you speak, think about the unspoken feelings and thoughts hidden within your seemingly neutral words. Visualize an Inner Triangle to remind you of your underlying purposes. Make an effort to express your feelings as well as your ideas.

2. *Think tip of the iceberg.* Visualize your words as only the tip of your mental and emotional iceberg. Think of all the circumstances and feelings concealed behind any statement you make. In your next conversation, practice tuning in to the feelings and purposes that lie behind your own statements.

3. *Interpret another person's Inner Triangle.* Select a minimum of three opportunities and develop your consciousness of another person's Inner Triangle. Whether you are involved in a simple conversation, an argument, or a business discussion, focus upon that other person. Ferret out the behind-the-scene mental and emotional activi-

ties at work. Read that person's body language. What does it tell
you? Ask the person, "What do you mean by that?" or "What is
your purpose in saying that?" "What is really on your mind?"
Reveal your own thoughts and feelings as an open and honest way
to bring the other person out. Go parallel and verbalize what you
think that other person is thinking. Delve deeper and try to make
contact with another person's Inner Triangle.

## Step 2: Eliciting the Bow Tie

1. *Get visual.* Draw the Bow Tie on a piece of paper. Cut out a
   model from a piece of cardboard. Etch it in your mind. Next time
   you are embroiled in a conversation, use the visual image of the
   Bow Tie to remind yourself that communication consists of two
   unique human beings pouring out their own personal meanings into
   the moment.

2. *Summarize.* Listen to what someone is saying to you. Before you
   respond and make your own point, summarize aloud what you
   think is happening within that other person's Inner Triangle. Present
   his or her case before presenting your own. Notice how this helps
   you focus on the other person.

3. *Be open.* We all fall into routines and patterns, but that doesn't
   mean we should close our minds, either to ourselves or to others.
   Are you open-minded? Are you willing to listen to a person express
   his or her particular point of view, even though you already have a

set opinion? Try it for the next few days. Think of the Bow Tie and try to open up your mind and your ears so that you really listen to your spouse or your co-worker or your friend and see them in a new light.

4. *Shift focus.* The next time you're trying to make a point and you don't seem to be getting through, try shifting the focus and emphasis of your conversation. Move from facts to feelings. Express how you feel about your subject and why it is so important to you. Or, shift to meanings and purposes, emphasizing what the subject means to you and your purpose in trying to persuade the other person.

5. *Get persuasive.* Think of someone whom you have to "sell" something to, whether it be a product, a business plan, or the idea of a raise and promotion. In planning for the conversation, remember to base your approach upon what you know about that other person —his or her feelings, fears, ambitions. When the time comes, listen carefully to what's going on behind his or her words and adjust your approach accordingly. Forget trying to be objective. Use your own Inner Triangle to make contact with the other person's Inner Triangle.

6. *Let your feelings talk.* Too often we hide behind our words and use them to disguise our real feelings. Go out of your way to express and verbalize your feelings for one whole day. Break through the barriers between you and another person by paying attention to Inner Triangles. Reach out to someone as a feeling, sentient human being. Take a chance. Make contact. Let your real, inner self emerge. You may discover a new "you" and so will your friends, business associates, family, and loved ones.

*part* 3

FORWARD

MOMENTUM

*t   e   n*

# THE TOOLS FOR LIVING WORK SHEET

The goal of the Inner Fitness Program is to provide us with the skills to 1) create opportunities for personal choice in our lives and 2) generate the emotional strength needed to help us actualize our dreams. These goals can be achieved only if we make the Tools an integral part of our lives. Just as we've made exercise and proper nutrition a part of our daily routine to keep physically fit, so must we make the Tools for Living a part of our personal regimen to become mentally and emotionally fit.

But how do we go about applying the Tools to our lives on an ongoing basis?

By keeping the six Tools at our fingertips and recalling their messages whenever we are faced with a problem, a sticky situation, or an emotional crisis. By practicing on our minor internal conflicts so that we can be more proficient in handling major crises. By doodling the visual images of the Tools to jog our minds and open ourselves to more imaginative solutions. By using the Work Sheet described below to help us search out fresh and creative approaches to living. And by returning to them again and again when specific needs arise.

Each Tool purposefully overlaps and reinforces the others. The consciousness of choosing instilled by the Circle and Dot might be aroused by Elmer's Glue, since delaying our responses cuts us loose from thinking in terms of the obvious or the traditional. The warning of the Bells is echoed in the positive message of the North Star. Responding to the Clock attunes us to see changes in another person and so helps us to utilize the communication process of the Bow Tie.

In practicing Inner Fitness, try applying the Tools one by one, in order, to a particular problem, utilizing what I call the Tools for Living Work Sheet. This entails listing all six Tools on one side of a piece of paper in order and then, one by one, applying each Tool to the problem at hand. Or the Work Sheet can be used following a conflict as a kind of therapy to help you work out and understand a difficult situation in a new light. This kind of systematic approach introduces a dynamic development to your appraisal, allowing you to find creative solutions to nagging problems.

With practice and conditioning, using the exercises at the end of each chapter and thinking daily of the different messages, the Tools will become internalized. They will become a natural, even unconscious, part of our decision-making process. Instead of actually seeing the image of the Circle and Dot, we will become conditioned spontaneously to keep an open mind when considering options. Over a period of time, the Tools will fuse to become a creative attitude that generates a new way of thinking.

Let's look at how the Tools work together as an interrelated system. The first two examples show how the Tools can be applied through a Work Sheet. Two case histories follow, utilizing a variety of Tools.

## WORK SHEET CASE 1: SANDRA K.

In Chapter 9 I told the story ("Let's Dance") of Sandra K., a fashion magazine editor who attended an industry dinner with her husband. Because she deemed it important to her career that she maintain a high profile at the dinner, she insisted that her often emotionless husband, Freddie, dance with her rather than sit glum and standoffish at the table. When he said he hated the music and didn't feel like dancing, they began bickering and Sandra finally stormed out of the ballroom. That night at home, they quarreled bitterly.

In the previous chapter, we explained how the Bow Tie could have helped this couple work through their insensitivity and defuse their conflict. In fact, the day after the quarrel, I met with Sandra, who was distraught about the blowup with her husband. I reviewed the Living Tools with her and asked her to apply them, using the Work Sheet. Her Work Sheet analysis shows how she used all the Tools for Living to help her understand, work through, and find some solutions to her particular problem and the underlying, ongoing friction she'd been having with her spouse. Notice the change in the focus and development of Sandra's feelings and thoughts as she works through the difficulty using the Tools.

**Elmer's Glue:**  When I put a Drop of Elmer's on my lips, the flow of angry words subsides. I pause and try to get hold of myself. I stop myself from blaming Freddie, from assuming I know what's going on, from rationalizing my anger. I close my eyes and become silent, opening myself to fresh feelings and insights. My deep love for Freddie resurfaces. Maybe I'm partly to blame. Maybe I'm too concerned with appearances. I want to work out a solution. I apply two Drops of Elmer's, take a deep breath, and feel my hard edges begin to soften. I concentrate on feeling rather than thinking. My sensitivity increases. My usual, straight-laced, businesslike perspective begins to open up and I see things in a larger perspective.

**The Bells:** At the moment I urged Freddie to dance, I heard my Bells ringing. I'd seen his face. I knew his mood. I had a gut feeling what was going to happen. Yet I'd ignored the warning signs. Had I actually wanted to provoke an argument? Was it possible that the violence of my reaction was caused by my own mixed feelings about the event, by my own guilt about wanting to show off before my peers and superiors? Or was I feeling hostile simply because Freddie made me feel guilty for my success? Was he simply being unreasonable and selfish, or was I taking my own anger out on him?

**The Circle and Dot:** Obviously this problem has nothing to do with dancing. What's the real problem? What Circles should I be setting up? The main Circles seem to revolve around his ongoing problem with the success of my career and my unhappiness with his recent lack of warmth and emotion. What are my options? Divorce. Separation. Extramarital affair. But I love Freddie. Vacation. Second honeymoon. A frank discussion of our problems. Keep adding Dots. Marriage counselor. Career counselor. Maybe that's it. Maybe the root of our problem lies in Freddie's unhappiness with his own job. For years he's been frustrated with his work and I've been too wrapped up in my own career to see just how it has affected him and our relationship. If I encourage him to seek out a new and challenging job, maybe we can get over this hump.

**The North Star:** I have a long-term dream. That someday Freddie and I can get out of the rat race and own our own business together in the country. We have the right experience. All we need is the capital. Then we could start a family. Maybe I should talk to him about this, start making some plans, start saving. Maybe we can explore our mutual fascinations and decide on just what kind of business we should have. We both love antiques. We both love country inns. If we share a dream and work toward it together, we're sure to become closer and more harmonious.

**The Clock:** I feel insecure. I depend upon Freddie and seek his approval. Yet these are old feelings, a carryover from an earlier stage in our relationship. When we met, he was a senior and I was a freshman in college. I saw him as someone to look up to, someone full of wisdom and self-confidence. He was an intellectual and I admired his rational, logical approach to the world. I'm not the same person anymore, though, and neither is he. $Sandra_{1990}$ and $Freddie_{1990}$ are very different from $Sandra_{1980}$ and $Freddie_{1980}$. We're equals now. I now see that he can be opinionated and insecure. He has trouble expressing his emotions, just like his father.

Recently, our sex life has been sporadic and not what it used to be. I've been assuming this was natural after ten years of marriage. Maybe, though, it's a result of changes in our relationship and growing anger at each other. Possibly, I should set a Time Span for renewing our marriage vows and actualizing our dream, so that we have something concrete to aim for.

**The Bow Tie:**   Why did Freddie refuse to dance? What was in his Inner Triangle, hidden behind the surface words of his refusal? I try to imagine the world from Freddie's point of view. Possibly, his ego was bruised. Not only had I requested he accompany me to the dinner, but I spent most of the evening table-hopping. Wasn't that insensitive? It seemed like such a trivial request but, obviously, it wasn't so trivial in Freddie's mind. Funny, after all these years, I'm suddenly not so sure that I really know him.

By working through the Living Tools Work Sheet, Sandra came to several important realizations and made several realistic plans of action. She became more aware of the strain under which Freddie was living. She dealt with the conflicts her career was causing by encouraging Freddie to pursue alternative job options in order to alleviate his own frustrations. And she took the first steps toward fulfilling their ultimate dream when Freddie and she took a vacation in the country. They looked at antiques shops and country inns, and made some long-term plans. On their return, Freddie made an appointment to see a head-hunter. Sandra promised not to drag him to any more affairs unless absolutely necessary, and he promised to take her dancing on Saturday night.

## WORK SHEET CASE 2:
## AN INVESTMENT
## OPPORTUNITY

I was recently approached by Steven T. with a proposal to invest in a new business venture. The concept involved a new medium for coupon advertising—placing coupon offers on the back of the register tape at the supermarket check-out counter. Steven and his partner, Tom L., pitched the idea to me and convinced me that they had worked out most of the technical problems. They had already excited the interest of numerous advertisers.

The idea seemed sound. The risk-reward ratio was excellent. And I began to think about all the opportunities for expansion and franchising. Intrigued by the idea, and on the verge of making a substantial investment, I decided to talk myself through the Living Tools Work Sheet before making a decision.

**Elmer's Glue:** Here I am, thinking of ways in which this coupon venture can expand, be set up on a franchise basis, go public, even be acquired, and I haven't yet decided whether to invest or thought through the implications of that investment. I must remember my own words: an empty mind is the beginning of wisdom. I apply a Drop of Elmer's Glue in order to stop the flow of words. The dust begins to settle. I realize that I've been working on the hidden assumption that if something makes sense, then it's worth doing. But that doesn't always follow. I've allowed my business mind to run away with my thinking. I must open the channels to my spiritual, feeling side. I decide to apply two Drops of Glue and meditate.

**The Bells:** I listen for my Bells and hear them ringing. I go through the list and realize that I'm hearing the sound of my Personal Weakness Bells. I'm doing it again—playing the sucker for a creative idea. If I'm not careful, I'll be in over my head before I know it. Then I receive a strong message from my Sixth Sense Bells. I realize that I have some deep, unfocused reservations about Tom. Although he is bright, I'm not sure I trust him. I'm not sure we could work together comfortably. The Work Sheet is beginning to open my channels.

**The Circle and Dot:** If I were actively searching for places to speculate, there are numerous options open to me. I could reconsider some of the venture capital deals that Larry B. has been pressing me to enter. I could set into motion one of my own business ideas—I have a storehouse of those. Better yet, I could back an off-Broadway play or produce my own musical. The opportunity to back Steven and Tom is only one Dot in a Circle, one answer to a problem. Although the idea is intriguing, it's an answer to a problem that I don't have. I'm not looking for a speculative venture at this time.

**The North Star:**  When I muse upon the North Star and allow my softer side to emerge and express itself, I realize that this venture has nothing to do with following my fascination. I am seeing dollar signs in the sky instead of my North Star. That compromise might have made sense years ago, but now it only arouses feelings of stress. I must remain true to myself. I can't afford to slip back into old patterns. Although this is a great opportunity to make money, it would undoubtedly swallow up enormous amounts of my time and energy. But I've been happily devoting myself to writing and music. Why should I follow someone else's fascination when I can continue to follow my own?

**The Clock:**  I am not the same person I was twenty years ago. Victor Dishy$_{1990}$ is not Victor Dishy$_{1970}$. My needs and goals have changed. I think I'm appraising this proposal using yesterday's yardstick. I am thinking as if I were back in the business world but Priorities$_{1990}$ are not Priorities$_{1970}$. And what about the Ripple Effect? If I do plunge into this venture, it will lead me deeper and deeper back into business, and this isn't where I want to go at this point in my life.

**The Bow Tie:**  Reviewing my meetings with Steven and Tom, I realize that I have sensed something in their Inner Triangles that I find disturbing. They are young, headstrong, ambitious—perhaps overly so. I sense that they will need to be reined in; that I will have to stay on them. I sense that I will find the relationship taxing and troublesome.

Having gone through the Living Tools Work Sheet, my decision crystallized almost instantly. I decided to pass on the offer. The decision felt right. I no longer felt stressed or anxious. The venture had all the signs of a major money maker but if we want to use the Living Tools to create a lifestyle, we have to know when to say, "No."

## CASE HISTORY 1: ABBE K.

Abbe K. has worked as a copywriter at Ogilvy and Mather in New York City for the past four years. She lives alone in a one-bedroom, rent-stabilized apartment off Gramercy Park. Although Abbe loves her job and her friends, she is lonely and tired of the city. She's sick of the bar scene and spends her weekends running errands, working, and going to the movies by herself. When a headhunter calls her about a position as associate creative director of a small agency in San Diego, she thinks, What the hell, and goes on the interview. The meeting goes well and she's asked to the Coast for further interviews. Now she's been offered the job and has till Monday morning to decide what to do.

Having been trained in Inner Fitness, Abbe applies the various Tools for Living to her situation. She hears the sound of her "I'm Trapped" Bells warning her that she's stagnating. At thirty-five, she's afraid that her youth is slipping away and that she's working her fingers to the bone but ending up with nothing to show for it. She isn't saving much money and has no love life to speak of; she seems stuck in a rut. Still, the thought of moving is frightening. No more seeing her best friends Jan and Marcie, no more Pete's Tavern, no more of her familiar routine. Will her furnishings re-create the same comfortable Gramercy Park atmosphere in San Diego? Will she like her new job? Will she make friends? Will she like the laid-back West Coast? What if it doesn't work out, then what?

Abbe thinks of the North Star and tries to pinpoint her dream. What really fascinates her? What does she want more than anything in the world? She hears the answer loud and clear from deep inside her: she wants to have a baby. Her biological clock is ticking and she wants a child, whether or not she has a husband. The idea of raising a child alone in New York City has always seemed impractical and daunting. Raising a child in San Diego in a house, maybe near the beach, seems much more possible.

Then the image of the North Star begins to sparkle in her mind's eye. She realizes that up to this point she has been thinking only in terms of the practicality of the move. Immersed in details, she has ignored her larger, spiritual urges. Her North Star is beckoning her to rekindle the passion of her life. Maybe in San Diego she could find the time to start that novel she's contemplated all these years.

Abbe thinks of the Circle and Dot but realizes that this is no time to search for another option. That's just a way of putting off the decision. Instead, she begins obsessing about the decision to the point where she has an anxiety fit. The pros and the cons of the situation become a mish-mash. She starts eating Ben & Jerry's ice cream to alleviate her anxiety, but this only makes her feel worse about herself. Finally, she applies a Drop of Elmer's Glue between her lips, stops thinking irrationally and compulsively, and pauses to catch her emotional breath.

She visualizes her little girl. She'll call her Amanda, and she'll have dark blond curly hair and a turned-up nose. She sees them walking hand and hand along the beach or in a clean, warm city without New York's hard edge of cynicism. Abbe goes on with her visualization, imagining herself tan and healthy, meeting new people, getting into the easy California lifestyle.

Suddenly, she applies two Drops of Elmer's Glue and drifts into a deeper inner silence. She reaches a state of harmony. Her deepest, most passionate self emerges. Without putting it into words or stating reasons, she *feels* that the move is a right one. Only after that experience does she verbalize her feeling: "I may never have this chance again. I don't know if I'll be better off, but I've got to take the risk and find out."

The Clock comes to mind, reinforcing her decision, reminding her that she is a changing person with changing needs. New York has been right for her until now, but now she is more concerned about quality of life and quality time than success or money. San Diego seems much more suited to her higher-level goals. At worst, if the job doesn't work out, she can always return to New York, especially if she only sublets her apartment. Maybe she'll even meet a man in San Diego. Maybe the job will give her new creative opportunities and the chance to make a lot of money.

Once again her Bells ring, alerting her to action. She thinks of what will happen if she turns down the job: another Monday morning at the office going through yet another creative meeting with the same staff, fighting with the same clients, and coming home to the same apartment. The offer, though, has already opened her eyes, stimulated her and changed her perspective. Now she senses that *not* making a move, staying put, is life-threatening. She accepts that the stress of relocating is merely the price of grasping new opportunities, and that while discomfort is temporary, regret is forever. Abbe makes up her mind: she takes the job.

# CASE HISTORY 2 : JOYCE H.

For the past four years, Joyce H., an attractive thirty-one-year-old photographer with sparkling brown eyes, has been living with Jason S., a slim, bearded thirty-five-year-old who is struggling to publish his first novel.

In the beginning, Joyce found the relationship exciting and stimulating. Although Jason was wrapped up in his writing, self-centered, and frequently angry, Joyce treated him with love and understanding. She liked living with a writer and indulged Jason and his "artistic temperament," knowing how difficult writing was and how desperately Jason wanted to succeed.

After four years, though, the bloom has faded. Joyce hasn't been working at her photography and feels useless and unloved. She is racked with self-doubt and feels as if she has been stagnating in Jason's shadow. At this point, she is exposed to the Inner Fitness Program.

Visualizing the Bow Tie, Joyce takes a close look at the inner dynamics of her life with Jason. "This relationship is just nonfunctional. I feel as if I've been on a treadmill, and in a trance for the past four years. I don't have any control over my life; I do whatever he tells me. God, I'm furious! I guess I'm just not ready to live a nice life. Or maybe I don't deserve it."

Suddenly, Joyce recognizes that her need for Valium, her constant constipation, and her insomnia are physical signs of her Bells ringing. Thanks to Inner Fitness, she begins to realize that the only way to rid herself of negative drives is to reach out for the positive. She hears the sound of the Bells as a warning of a life-threatening danger. Realizing that she can no longer afford the psychological luxury of exploring and dissecting her past, she begins to take charge of her life.

She comes across an old clipping about the MacDowell Colony, an elite artist's colony in New Hampshire where artists in different fields are invited to spend two weeks living and working together in a creative environment. Although Joyce has studied photography, and has a portfolio of her own material, she has let her talent slide as she submerged her ego to Jason's needs. She realizes that, for years, she has been neglecting her North Star, but now she feels a tiny, bright flame beginning to burn inside her. For once, she will follow her fascination. The Circle and Dot comes to mind and the yellowing newspaper clipping suddenly turns into a fresh new option—an opportunity to awaken her creativity and control her destiny.

Joyce applies to MacDowell and, to her surprise, is accepted; she is taken seriously as an artist for the first time in her life. "Imagine, *I* have talent!" she says to herself. Acting on her Bells, she has made things happen. Her North Star shines brightly. Following her fascination has released torrents of positive energy. She now feels much better about herself and opens herself up to pursuing a new path in her life.

Returning to her cramped city apartment, Joyce applies a Drop of Elmer's Glue, thus ending her role playing and predictable responses, and opening herself to seek out creative solutions. Without knowing quite why or being able to articulate her action (and without any decision about whether she will continue to live with Jason), she starts looking for a new apartment. She merely senses that this is the right thing to do. Conditioned to use the Tools for Living, she begins to be more fearful of _not_ acting than of acting; a change, any change, seems better than the status quo. Little by little, she begins to adopt the "I Choose" lifestyle.

When Joyce learns of the death of her forty-year-old cousin, killed during an armed robbery of his Greenwich Village lamp store, she envisions the image of the Clock and realizes that life is short, that there's no time to waste. She looks back on the last four years and asks herself: "Do I want to go on this way? Is this the future I want for myself?"

A few weeks later, she finds her own apartment, breaks from Jason, and devotes herself to her photography. Within a very short time, her

# MOVING
# FORWARD

I nner Fitness is, in essence, a hands-on program that urges us first to listen to our dreams and our instincts and then to create realistic plans to actualize those dreams and act on those instincts. It urges us to get out of the office and into the field, and to develop our perceptions and plans solidly, meticulously, from the ground up. For only by tempering instincts with facts and firsthand experience can we take our best shot at accomplishing our goals.

But there is more to this hands–on philosophy and to being operational than the practical edge it provides us: it entails seeing the extraordinary in the ordinary. It means agreeing with Albert Einstein when he says, "God is in the details." Listen to the words of the painter, Antoni Tapies, who offers a poignant description of what it means to see the world through the eyes of someone who sees the magic in little things:

"Look at the simplest object. Look, for example, at an old chair. It does not seem to be much. But think about the whole universe that it contains: the hands and the sweat of the person who carved the wood which was once a robust tree, full of energy, in the middle of a thick forest high up in the mountains; the loving work of the person who built it; the pleasure of the person who bought it; the pains and joys which it probably supported in a great living room, or maybe in a poor dining room in a working class suburb. All, absolutely all of that represents life and has importance. Even the oldest chair carries in it the sap which, far away in the forest, rose from the earth and which will still serve to give heat the day when, having become mere pieces of wood, it will burn in a fireplace."

The next time we find ourselves looking at a person we have known for years, remember what Antoni Tapies sees in a chair. Really look at this other person. Focus upon what makes that person special. Sense and feel the dreams and desires that have slipped away. The pleasures he or she has enjoyed. The sorrows. The inner battles. The lovers and enemies. See this person on an operational level by seeing through the eyes of an artist.

## LIVING WITH PROBABILITIES

A commitment to action is not made any easier when we face the reality: there are no guarantees in life, only probabilities! We can never be sure how our decisions will turn out. Because the world inside and around us never stands still, we must learn to deal in probabilities rather than in guarantees.

Seeking absolute certainty in life is a surefire way to short-circuit our entire decision-making machinery. Even the Tools for Living are not 100 percent accurate: sometimes our Bells are wrong and sometimes the Dot we select from the Circle of options isn't the cure-all for our problems.

Dealing with an uncertain and risky world requires a skill somewhat like riding a bicycle: we achieve stability only by constantly making imperceptible adjustments. We "go with the flow," as the saying goes, continually shifting our position to fit the demands of a process-oriented world. When solving a problem, we apply a trial-and-error technique that involves an ongoing process of probing and correcting. To operate at maximum efficiency in a world where certainty is illusory, we must avoid searching for nonexistent, perfect solutions.

## THE EMOTIONAL LEAP

Merely accepting the absence of certainty in the world isn't always enough to make us move. Sometimes, like Hamlet, we find ourselves stalled and immobilized by our own rationalizing. We create a wonderful playground for doubts and end up undermining our most detailed plans. Leaning too heavily upon reason as our guide, we analyze and weigh our options but never take action.

> **The major obstacle in the path of creative, positive movement is the belief that a decision is a purely rational matter.**

The truth is that no matter how carefully we prepare, every decision requires an emotional commitment. Because of the absence of certainty, we can never be 100 percent sure whether we are right or what the consequences of our decision will be; therefore, when we act, our rational calculation must include our emotional calculation. In other words, we must consider our feelings, our intuition, along with our perceptions of the facts of the situation. An emotional spark is needed to turn thought into action, to give us the psychic energy to commit ourselves to carrying out our decision.

> **At the point of taking action, all decisions become emotional leaps.**

Although careful thinking gives us an edge and prepares us to move, we must have faith in ourselves and the self-confidence to make that move. Realizing this is the key to breaking the mental log jam caused by fear or passivity. Building this confidence and emotional resolve has been one of the principal goals of the Inner Fitness Program.

Even Bernard Baruch, respected advisor to presidents and wizard of Wall Street, when asked for the secret behind his financial success, said that he gathered all the facts he could, then plunged. Because we can only deal in probabilities and because sound thinking can only bring us to the brink of a decision, ultimately all actions are nothing more than tests of our emotional courage.

## TURN LIVING
## INTO AN ART FORM

With proper care, living can be elevated from a skill into an art. Just as a sculptor molds a piece of clay, or an artist, brushstroke by brushstroke, creates a painting, so do we, with every action we take and every decision we make, create our own lives—our own living works of art. With the sensitivity of an artist we soon come to realize that each day is a fresh start, a new adventure, and a new opportunity for creativity.

Every day, of course, will not be a masterpiece. Just as an artist discards many sketches, so may we wish to throw away some difficult, frustrating days. Fortunately, a few beautiful days can last a lifetime, especially if major turning points that shape and direct our lives occur on those days. Just as there is no one "best" artistic style or technique, so there is no one "perfect" way to create our lives. The options are infinite—as infinite as the opportunities we seize to make an "I Choose" life.

We have reached the end of the Inner Fitness Program. Piece by piece we have assembled a workable design for living life more fully.

Used consistently and wisely, the Living Tools described in this book will enable us to develop the skills needed to embrace the "I Choose" lifestyle, a lifestyle devoted to enhancing our opportunities for personal expansion and free choice in our social, private, and career worlds. Like the chair Antoni Tapies describes, we contain a universe within us. It is my profound wish that Inner Fitness will bring that universe to life for each of us and make our time on this earth an ongoing, creative work of art.

**BOOKMARK**

The text of this book was set in the typeface Bembo
by Berryville Graphics, Berryville, Virginia.

It was printed and bound by Berryville Graphics,
Berryville, Virginia.

DESIGNED BY CHRIS WELCH

Printed in the United States
by Baker & Taylor Publisher Services